This book is for
JOCELIN WINTHROP YOUNG
Founder Director

In September, 2005, Round Square presented a "Scroll of Honour" to its Founder Director, which read as follows:

He translated an educational philosophy into energetic and effective reality. His dedication, enthusiasm and organisational skills created a global movement that has enriched the lives of thousands of students and teachers. . .

To him we owe the ever-growing existence of an association that has brought challenge and fulfillment to the young, hope and help to those in need, and a real sense of vision to all who encounter its ideals.

IDEALS AT WORK

EDUCATION FOR WORLD STEWARDSHIP IN THE ROUND SQUARE SCHOOLS

Peter Tacy

DEERFIELD ACADEMY PRESS

DEERFIELD, MASSACHUSETTS

IDEALS at Work
*Education for World Stewardship
in the Round Square Schools*

Peter Tacy

Illustrations for this book are not provided in printed form, but are available on-line at www.roundsquare.org/idealsatwork.htm.
Participants in Round Square projects or other activities who wish to make photos available for use as future illustrations are invited to send these, as digital files, with complete text explanations, to webmaster@roundsquare.org.

Copies of *IDEALS at Work* are available from www.roundsquare.org.

Editor: Andrea Moorhead
Design: Robert Moorhead
Copy Editors: Janet MacFadyen & Rosalie Pratt

ISBN: 0-9755758-2-1
Deerfield Academy Press
7 Boyden Lane   Deerfield, Massachusetts 01342

© 2006 Peter Tacy

PRINTED IN THE UNITED STATES OF AMERICA
SPRINGFIELD PRINTING, NORTH SPRINGFIELD, VERMONT

CONTENTS

FOREWORD 7
Eric Widmer

PREFACE 9

CHAPTER 1:
A First Look at Round Square and a Visit to Three Schools 15
St. Philip's College, Athenian School, Starehe Boys' Centre & School

CHAPTER 2:
Round Square — the First Half Century 36

CHAPTER 3:
"IDEALS" at Work 63

CHAPTER 4:
Three More Schools — 93
Appleby College, St. Cyprian's School, The Doon School

CHAPTER 5:
Improving the World, One Student at a Time 113

CHAPTER 6:
Students and Graduates Assess Round Square 129

CHAPTER 7:
A Final Three Schools — 144
Schüle Schloss Salem, Deerfield Academy, Gordonstoun School

CHAPTER 8:
Being Challenged, and Needed 168

APPENDIX A:
Additional Resources 177

APPENDIX B:
    Teaching Character, Judgement, and Courage   179
    HRH Prince Andrew, Duke of York

APPENDIX C:
    Contributors   183

APPENDIX D:
    Survey Form   187

LIST OF ROUND SQUARE SCHOOLS   189

Foreword

The possibility of a book about Round Square has been the happy result of a conjunction of circumstances. First of all, the Round Square organization had to have the idea — a simple enough proposition, it would seem, but not really so. Round Square is such a public spirited, service-dedicated organization that the thought of a book about itself would never have occurred, except for a second circumstance. And that was the availability of someone to write it.

When Peter Tacy was confronting the issue of his retirement his situation was quite vulnerable (as I know for myself), and it was exactly the right time to take up with him the plan of writing a book about Round Square. Everything about Peter made him the perfect choice: the fact that he graduated from a Round Square school (Deerfield), that he had spent his life in independent secondary education, and that if he took on the job, we knew that he would do it, and do it beautifully.

A third circumstance was the knowledge that we had a ready publisher in the Deerfield Academy Press, under the dedicated stewardship of Andrea and Robert Moorhead. Now the result is in our hands, and the Round Square story is told for all to read and hear and re-tell and preserve for those students, long into the future, who will want to know the history of this proud and purposeful organization, and who will be thrilled, as we are, that it is a story that has been told so well.

Eric Widmer
Head of School, Deerfield Academy
June 6, 2006

*Round Square
is a world-wide association of schools
which share a commitment, beyond
academic excellence, to personal development
and responsibility through service,
challenge, adventure, and international
understanding…empowering
students to become the
leaders and guardians of
tomorrow's world.*

Preface

TELL STORIES! (Advice from a student in India)

This book is only in part a work by an educator about his professional interests. And while it contains original research, it cannot claim to be a scholarly essay — I have been far too deeply involved with the organization which is the book's subject to present myself as a dispassionate observer. Long before this book was undertaken, I came to respect the aims of Round Square, and to see it as a model of good practice which merits understanding and replication. So this is not a scholar's book. Rather, it is offered by a believer.

What you are about to read also includes statements, recollections, and assessments which represent the voices of a great many individuals — primarily secondary-level students attending Round Square schools, and graduates of these schools. These statements are without exception honest. In many cases, though, they go past mere candor to reflect passionate enthusiasm and conviction. Read these words, then, as messages from young people around the world who were motivated to speak because they felt personally driven to share insights gained through their own experience.

These comments also reflect only a fraction of a population. While I received questionnaire responses from more than nine hundred members of this global community of students and graduates (see Chapter Six), that number — more than significant for research purposes — is still but a small percentage of the total number of students and graduates of Round Square schools. Similarly, the "profiles" of nine schools (Chapters One, Four, and Seven) speak only of those nine institutions — which are half the number I visited while preparing this book, and about a seventh of all Round Square member schools. The nine were chosen not because they are "better" than others, or because I am particularly fond of them, but simply because they offered what seemed to be a useful range of school types and locales, length of Round Square involvement, and other interesting contrasts. There is, in fact, *no* Round Square school which would have been unworthy of my examination — or of yours!

For these reasons, but above all out of respect for the worth of the views and insights of those who happened *not* to be heard, I suggest this book should be seen more as an introduction to Round Square than as the last word about it. Or — better yet — think of it as *story-telling*.

That's not an apology. As students at several schools reminded me, telling stories really *does* have value, especially for the young. When we are young, we need to hear — and tell — stories, especially stories about adventures and the discoveries adventure can offer. We need them in order to puzzle out who we are, what is expected of us, and what we may become.

The stories students told me about themselves, and asked me to pass along to others, were invariably seen by them as important — stories aimed not just at relating experience, but at revealing what had been uncovered — the *truth*. The story of Round Square is also an adventure story. It too points to understandings which seem to be true.

I will of course welcome retellings, corrections, additions, and rebuttals, as well as alternate versions of fact. After all, that is part of the story-telling tradition.

§

My own involvement with Round Square formally began nearly twenty-five years ago. However, it was the flowering of seeds planted far earlier, by my family, and by mentors and teachers. I grew up in an extended family which entrusted a lot of responsibility to the young. They included us in their debates and discussions, took our own views seriously, and gave us each an opportunity to explore the world. But they expected a lot of us, too. That was, I've since learned, a pretty good way to prepare a young person for a useful life and, now that I think about it, for life in a democracy.

I was lucky enough to attend Deerfield Academy, which is now a Round Square school. That was in the early 1950's, before Round Square existed. However, Deerfield was a most unusual school even then, in ways which are by no means unrelated to its present Round Square membership. Deerfield made a profound impression on me, for which I will always be grateful.

I was lured for the first time into thinking about the role of experience in the development of the individual by Professor John Miller, while I was a student at Williams College. In particular, the encounter with Dewey which Miller brought about for me in a philosophy course left an indelible mark on my mind — although, as Miller was the first to tell me, such a fascination does not necessarily transform a curious undergraduate into a philosopher.

A far more powerful and lasting influence began in 1962 when I signed up to teach for a year at Buxton School in Massachusetts, which was then headed by its founder, Ellen Geer Sangster. Mrs. Sangster was cut from the same cloth as many of the figures you will meet in this book. She was an educational pioneer, and a true internationalist. Fascinated by each developing person she was educating, she was an intrepid promoter of adventure and self-discovery for each of those she educated. No young teacher could be plunged into one of Buxton's all-school field study / performance trips with Ellen Sangster literally at the head of the pack and emerge unaware of what a school could *really* take on, and what students could *really* accomplish. My year at Buxton became nineteen. By the time I left, my professional perspective was essentially complete.

I was happy enough to be led toward Round Square in 1981, just after I became a Head of School, by my friend Steve Davenport, who was then Head of Athenian School in California. The connection with Round Square which formed was immediate, and has only grown more deeply-rooted with the passage of time. Before long I was President of the short-lived "Okanela Conference" of North American schools which was eventually absorbed in an expanding Round Square. I headed a Round Square member school, and later served for nine years on the Round Square Board. I am still listed as an Honorary Member of Round Square.

Through all these connections I came to know, respect, and care for Round Square's Founder Director, Jocelin Winthrop Young, and for his outstanding successor, Terry Guest. I also developed a deep respect and affection for the Chair of the Board, King Constantine of Greece, for the long-serving Coordinator of RSIS (the Round Square International Service), Ann West, and the organization's first Secretary, Kay Holland. With each of these five persons I share that special kind of friendship which arises not just from shared beliefs, but from shared *work* in the service of commonly held beliefs. I treasure these ties.

Many other women and men with whom I have shared involvement with Round Square have been kind enough to encourage me in the development of this book. I cannot thank them sufficiently. I would especially like to acknowledge the aid and encouragement of Gulab Ramchandani, Dyke Brown, David Byatt, Goetz Plessing, and the Duke of York, Prince Andrew, who has been kind enough to allow a portion of a talk he gave about Round Square to be included (see Appendix B).

Assistance came my way from several Heads of Round Square schools, all of whom I am proud to call friends. These include but are not limited to Eleanor Dase, Guy McLean, Stephen Higgs, Brian Dawson, Kanti Bajpai, Alan Ross, Brian Simons, Stephen Lowry, Bernhard Bueb, Eric Widmer, Chris Tudor, Marion Farndale, Mark Pyper, Tessa Fairbairn, and Rod Fraser. Widmer was kind enough to supply the introduction to this volume, and to arrange for its publication.

Four others, beloved friends and colleagues, were valued sources of encouragement and friendship. All are now gone. In my heart I nevertheless feel a need to thank each of them — Roy McComish, Peter Pelham, Alan Patterson, and Geoffrey Griffin.

The travel required for this book was funded by gifts made through Friends of Round Square / USA by Steve and Mary Smith and by Steve and Joanna Davenport; and through Friends of Round Square / Canada, by Appleby College. I was lodged as I visited schools by Brian Simons, Sue Patterson, Wendy and Bertie Kerr, Ian and Elaine McLachlan, Geoffrey Griffin, Kay Holland, Eleanor and John Dase, Steve and Joanna Davenport, Eric Widmer, Guy and Joanne McLean, Terry and Sue Guest, Jocelin Winthrop Young and his daughter Sophie Weidlich, Mark and Jenny Pyper, Chaviva Hosek and Alan Pearson, and Gulab and Ratna Ramchandani, as well as through arrangements provided by St. Philip's College, Stanford Lake College, and St. Cyprian's School.

Many RS Reps met, aided, encouraged, and sustained me. Among that group — all people who are essential in maintaining the strength and the character of Round Square — I especially want to thank Peter Cole, John O'Shea, Andrew Fox, Rod Summerton, Sarah Pollitt, Wendy Kerr, Joan Buckley, Bridget Painter, Jenn Wallace, David Carr, Peter Ndungu, Martha Lyman, John Hamilton, Helen White, Maggie Chodak, Ulrike Niederhofer, Madhav Saraswat, Jayant Lal, Vishnu Painuli, Arnie Boyle, and Rob McGuinness. Alec McCubbin, a former RS Rep at Lakefield College School in Canada, not only led me through the snow to and from his school, but while enroute managed to lead me to my first-ever Great Grey Owl — a "life bird." That may not have been the greatest of the revelations which this project held for me, but it was not the least.

Many others offered guidance and encouragement, including Round Square staff members Jane Howison and Richard Poulton, and RS Reps whom I couldn't visit but were especially supportive, including Tony Hyde, Stephen Eardley, Pierina Redler, Emma Williams, Ernst Leube, and Tony Vintcent. Alan Wills at Gordonstoun, Sophie Weidlich at Salem, and Kay Holland were invaluable helpers in searching out archival documents and helping me understand who was who, and who did what / when. Steve

Davenport was a patient, careful, encouraging reader of this book in draft. Gulab Ramchandani, Jocelin Winthrop Young, and Terry Guest were kind enough to check the finished text for accuracy, and they also offered a wealth of useful advice. Bob and Andrea Moorhead were all that editors should be, and more. Much is owed to each of them for their help.

The statistical analysis for Chapter Six was performed by my beloved, wonderfully talented niece, Emma Buchtel, who is a doctoral student in Cultural Psychology at the University of British Columbia. Much of the less exotic but equally valuable work involved with tabulating and recording data from close to a thousand student and graduate questionnaires was made possible through many hours of assistance provided by my wife Barbara. For that help, and also for her endless patience and acceptance of the months I had to spend elsewhere while visiting schools — and for *everything* else — I owe her more than I can possibly relate.

§

Late in his life, Kurt Hahn (a somewhat reluctant godfather to Round Square) journeyed to California to give an address at the founding ceremonies for Athenian School, which had been created by his former Schüle Schloss Salem pupil, Dyke Brown.

Hahn's talk was less a conventional sort of address than a personal valedictory, a summing-up of the views and convictions he had formed over a lifetime. Nevertheless, he saw fit to conclude what was a very personal message not with his own words, but with a quotation from the historian George Trevelyan that may well serve as an *envoi* for this volume:

> *Two passions are not likely to die out of the world, the love of country and the love of freedom. They can be kept pure by one thing which can tame yet not weaken them, tender love of all mankind.*

Hahn's great gift was to understand the importance challenge plays in the full development of a young person, and to find ways to make meaningful challenge available to the young. When speaking to students, he tended to pose his challenges in stark moral terms. The most persistent of these precepts was the challenge for each young person to feel, and act on, a "tender love for all mankind," — or more succinctly, *compassion*.

> *Are you in earnest about the ideals you profess? Who shall give the answer? I say, {it is} young men and women ready to do as the good Samaritan has done.*

It is easy to see how Trevelyan's words suited Hahn's purpose as he spoke to — and challenged — Athenian's students on that November day in California, forty years ago.

The need for *compassionate citizens of the world* is no less urgent today. Meeting that need is the driving force behind the story of Round Square.

CHAPTER 1:
A First Look at Round Square and a Visit to Three Schools

IN THE SUMMER OF 1954, a trio of European schools — from Germany, Britain and Greece — sent a hundred student volunteers (citizens of eight countries) to the Greek island of Cephalonia to rebuild a home for the elderly which had been destroyed by an earthquake.

A service expedition was not an extraordinary project for any one of these schools to undertake. Each had always believed that students should find ways to help people in need and that outside-the-classroom learning and adventure as well as voluntary service should be seen as *important* parts of schooling. And the three schools were already, if informally, linked to each other through personal, professional, and historical connections.

But there were some novel circumstances. The project would last longer than typical service experiences organized by the schools. It would be a collaboration — no single school or school culture formed the project's expectations or its group ethos. It was aimed at a real and vital need: if it failed, a group of elderly people would be homeless. Unlike most service work the students had previously performed, this project would take place on unfamiliar ground, and would be shared with co-workers who would be strangers for the most part. The social organization of the group wasn't pre-ordained. Rather, the norms, expectations, and peer leadership of this diverse, multinational community of teenagers would have to be developed on the spot by the youngsters who were taking part. And above all, the task itself would be *hard* and physically challenging, as the living conditions on this normally impoverished and now devastated Greek island would be primitive.

Despite such formidable challenges, what transpired during the project astonished adult observers. A powerful, generous morale developed among the students and continued to grow. An extraordinary level of student investment in the task and a gradual empowerment of the student group in leading the whole undertaking was taking place. And it was clear that a major learning event had occurred.

The subsequent effort of the little group of adults who had seen all this happening to understand fully, and then recreate and sustain similar experiences for more students, was the original spark which led to what has become a global network of collaborating schools in eighteen nations. This community of like-minded institutions is called Round Square.

This book will examine Round Square in a number of ways. We will look at it as a historic development, as an ongoing international program, and as a movement which is clear in its objectives and remarkably tolerant of differences in how schools in different parts of the world pursue them. We will stop to look at examples of ways in which Round Square's aims are expressed by a variety of schools in sometimes sharply contrasting environments. We will also look at Round Square through the eyes of students and graduates of these schools. Not only have statements provided by these students and graduates been scattered throughout the text, but an entire chapter will review research about attitudes and values of the young people who are educated at these schools.

One might reasonably ask *why* Round Square merits such attention. After all, there are hundreds of millions of school-age children in the world. Round Square schools educate only 50,000 of them. Why is such a *small* subject worth *so much* attention? Four answers to this question leap to mind:

- In a rapidly globalizing world, it is increasingly understood that *all* competent secondary schools and school systems will need to find ways to move beyond narrow, "national" or traditionally defined curricula if they are to prepare today's young people to deal with the challenges they will face in their adult lives. Round Square, which has spent decades exploring how "national" schools can support student learning in a multi-national context, offers a proven model of how such a need can be addressed.

- Round Square presents an example of how an educational movement can grow powerfully and with cohesion, resilience, and staying power across national and cultural barriers *if* it operates not as a conventionally organized "non-governmental organization" but as a consensual, objectives-focused network. To borrow a phrase from the jargon of the high-tech world, Round Square is framed less as a normal organization than as a "distributed system" — or to use its own term, a "community of like-minded schools."

It is also interesting that Round Square's long-established form of organization not only has proved to be effective and durable, but is ideally suited to an Internet world — one in which schools, teachers, and students can use a cheap, accessible, quick and flexible resource to create and sustain a working community across vast distances. School leaders around the world are asking "where's the payoff?" for the investments they are making in new technology. Round Square provides a fascinating example of how a huge payoff can result if a school's human system aligns with the open structure of the Internet.

- The outcomes for students which are achieved by Round Square schools defy conventional expectations in exciting and provocative ways. Perhaps the most important of these surprises is the evident lack of a "zero sum" result when the core curriculum is invaded by what might be conventionally termed the "extra-curriculum." Sending kids off to do volunteer service or to be exchange students at schools in other parts of the world, inviting them to climb mountains or explore wilderness rivers, or asking them to devote time and energy to the support and management of their community, would seem to take them away from (and thus diminish their performance in) the "core curriculum." At school after school, however, it's reported that Round Square energizes learning in *all* parts of the curriculum.

Round Square demonstrates that schools (and an international organization of schools) in which students are asked to rise to personal challenges, take on real responsibilities, and better the lives of others need *not* lose the ability to focus on and excel at more traditional goals.

The emerging field of brain research is beginning to explain why this "no zero sum" aspect of Round Square actually works as it does (see Chapter Five for more on this subject). However, most of what Round Square schools have long demonstrated really needs no aid from cutting-edge science to challenge traditional ways of thinking about what secondary education "can" and "cannot," "must" and "must not" do.

- The most important reason to read this book is because Round Square powerfully demonstrates what may be achieved if we decide to *take young people more seriously as human beings* during the time we educate them.

Round Square schools succeed because they *respect* the young people they educate. They behave in a way which lets students know they are valued as people, and that their potential to make a positive difference in the world is respected. Students respond with courage, imagination, compassion, and self-respect.

Schools which capitalize on education having a respect for the worth and potential of each young person, and are willing to invest in the development of that potential as a central part of their programs, are likely to be seen as relevant and useful by those they teach. Students and graduates describe the consequence of education at a Round Square school by presenting a list which is almost always headed by the words "self discovery." Adult leaders often describe this as "empowerment." The difference in terms is merely one of perspective.

Round Square assumes that each teenager innately needs to discover and master the world beyond and within himself or herself. Schooling should not thwart that need, nor should it ignore it. Instead a school should respect this natural priority, and allow itself to be energized through helping students meet it. Each youngster merits support in his or her exploration beyond the familiar "comfort zone" to find evidence that he or she can indeed be a valuable, effective, dynamic, *good* person. For this reason, each student must be encountered as a human being upon whom a community, a society, and a world will depend. Each must come to see herself or himself as a person who is *needed, and as one who can meet needs.*

"You are needed" is the core message Round Square brings to youngsters.

The response of young people to this proposition, as you will see, is impressive.

§

It was only when I was put at odds against everything familiar to me — whether it be my home, my culture, my traditions or my language — that I truly learned about myself.
— Male student, USA

It's a late October morning in Alice Springs, Australia, close to the end of spring and the beginning of a long, scorching summer in this remote desert town. Even now the sun is hot. A wallaby moves slowly along in the rocky scrub, unwilling to exert more energy than absolutely necessary in the growing heat. Groups of parrots — Galahs and Port Lincoln ring-necks — cluster together wherever there are bits of shade. Nearby is a waterless "river" and on the horizon lie the jagged peaks of the Macdonnall Range. Beyond these and other nearby ridges are the vast Gibson, Simpson, Tanami and Great Victoria Deserts. And beyond *them*, by at least a thousand kilometers in any direction, are the outskirts of urbanized Australia.

It's close to the end of the school year at St. Philip's College, an independently governed secondary school in one of the world's more remote places, Alice Springs, Australia. St. Philip's, which is affiliated with Australia's Uniting Church, is the only independent, boarding / day university-prep school in the nation's vast mid-continental area. For years it has educated the sons and daughters of the small number of residents in this region — government employees, operators of cattle stations, outback enthusiasts, and Aboriginal people.

The inclination to sum things up, which seems to strike all kids at the end of a school year in every part of the world, has overtaken a group of St. Philip's students with whom I am speaking. They meet with me in the surprising coolness of a beautiful school building made of tamped earth, corrugated metal and glass — classic outback building materials — and leap at the chance to reflect on their experiences at St. Philip's. What they are discussing, though, is not the extraordinary natural environment of the school, or its equally extreme geographic isolation. Instead, they are talking about the "connectedness" of St. Philip's with a wide, fascinating, accessible world.

For all these students, education at St. Philip's has *not* just involved texts, labs, discussion, and exams at the school, plus life in Alice Springs. It has brought them into contact with their location, to be sure. They have all provided voluntary service in the Alice Springs community, have trekked in the mountains and the desert, and have studied the imperiled culture of the Aboriginal people who make up nearly half of the town's inhabitants. But their education has gone well beyond that. It has impelled them beyond St. Philip's, beyond "Alice," and the huge state called The Northern Territory — and beyond Australia. Their school has sent them away from all this for some period of time, and also away from the familiarities of nationality, class, race, language, and other social descriptors, to meet up with new experiences. As a result, what they want to talk about would, in many parts of the world, seem extraordinary just for teenagers to *imagine*, much less have done.

One girl talks of the challenge she faced as an exchange student — and particularly as a *female* exchange student — at a school in India. Learning how to understand, show respect for, and be accepted by her peers and their families was hard, she says; but it was also very hard to keep in mind that "being yourself is still okay." A boy talks about how the unexpected experience of befriending a small child while helping to rebuild a simple home in the child's impoverished Cape Town, South Africa, neighborhood deeply affected him. Another boy suggests that the exchange term he spent in Canada was more than just time to travel abroad: it was "a journey of self-discovery."

What I am hearing are not just teenagers' stories about tourism. These are reports from young people who have been exploring global society on a very personal level, and have been changed by the experience. The students talk about how they didn't just meet but "connected" with young people through work and study in other countries, and about how they found, through international voluntary service work, that "working together can really mean connecting at *depth*."

They report on situations in which they found unsuspected abilities and more courage than they had previously thought they possessed. The words they choose are striking: "opportunity, discovery, experience, connection, give, provide, enjoy." And they have also learned a few qualitative lessons, which sometimes need no detailed explanation. "Not *all* experience is valuable," murmurs one student. Heads nod in agreement. What they mean is that they've found that you rarely reach a higher goal than the one you dared to aim for. For any teenager, that's a huge — and golden — life lesson.

Another group of students, most of whom are a bit younger than the first batch, talk about the personal impact of receiving "exchangers" from other schools as well as exchanging oneself. Both experiences, they tell me, lead to one's thinking in new ways about diversity — not just diversity between nations and cultures, but *within* them. And all agree that they returned from their own exchange or service experiences with eyes that now were able to see their familiar school and locality in brand new ways.

"It opened up my mind," says one youngster. "I realized then that I didn't want to let myself be trapped in one way of life and one perspective." "Until then," another says, "I took this time in my life for granted. Now I've learned that I want to get what I *need* to get, and that I really *can* do it." A girl who'd studied in a country where the first language is not English found, to her relief, that her limited fluency in the local language "really needn't be a barrier" which would make an exchange unprofitable. Another remarks that, although she was "amazed at how diverse and complex" the culture of the country where she took part in a service project really was, the discovery of "human similarities" was just as stunning.

Later in the same day, I meet with three young St. Philip's graduates, all in their 20s. Knowing that I will be writing about their school, they are unabashed (but polite) in offering advice. One remarks that I must "keep it in mind [when writing about this aspect of St. Philip's] that *enjoyment* is important. This is *fun!*" "It's a *deeper* sort of fun that can come from doing good and brave things. You just don't forget lessons of this kind," I'm told.

All agree that the end product of education at this school is always more than mere knowledge, but "a more positive look on things." These statements aren't brash. However, they are made in a deeply affirmative, look-you-in-the-eye manner. The information is being presented not as a theory, but as *fact*.

The Head of the school, Chris Tudor, an energetic and earnest man, and his long-time Board chair, a surgeon, meet with me at the end of the day. Both are full of stories about the "fascinating transformations" in students which have happened as a result of the international and experiential nature of the St. Philip's program. Both see the expense of funds caused by this expansion of the school's program beyond the normal concept of "curriculum" as not just an added bit of enrichment, but as "an investment," one which has "helped the place become what it is" and which is, by now, "an integral part of this school."

Both say that the knowledge that other schools in the world are pursuing the same goals, and doing so in ongoing collaboration with St. Philip's, is of real importance to them, their staff, and their students. It's not just a matter of fellowship, the Head says, or of combating geographic isolation. Once you've admitted that you are all seeking similar objectives, the sort of collegiality they've all "invested" in tends to breed not just the affirmation that comes from shared vision, but a "friendly envy" which results in good ideas being quickly appraised by and, now and then, replicated at, schools around the globe. He says this with a bit of a twinkle in his eye. Clearly St. Philip's has picked up some good ideas from colleague schools. He also knows that his school has passed some good examples along.

§

It's the same season, spring, but a half-year later on the calendar, on the opposite side of the planet. Athenian School is, like St. Philip's, located in a dramatic part of the world's geography. Its collection of sturdy timber-framed, wide-eaved, low buildings (this is, after all, earthquake country) is placed at the foot of Mt. Diablo, in Danville, California, a half-hour's expressway drive east of San Francisco, traffic permitting. Behind the school is the mountain, a dominant skyline feature when one looks eastward from downtown San Francisco. Mt. Diablo slopes up, and up. What we see in its direction from the campus is a wild and lovely place, which has been preserved as a natural area by the State of California. Amid the park's oaks and evergreens, wild deer and boar are plentiful, and mountain lions are rumored to lurk. When the breeze is right, white-tailed kites can be seen from paths on the Athenian campus, soaring on updrafts. It's all quite stunning. In fact, if one only looks from the school's campus in the direction of Mt. Diablo, it's easy to imagine that what one is seeing is the wild (or at least, thinly settled) California which existed here less than two hundred years ago.

But on all other sides of the school there is a landscape which is a far cry from Mt. Diablo. What's there is not only a massive contrast to the desert environment and outpost-community ethos of Alice Springs, Australia, but is stunningly unlike the view toward the mountain. Here, in neighborhoods named Diablo and Blackhawk, there is *upper*-up-market suburban housing. It extends as far as the eye can see — tasteful, beautifully tended, and expensive. The area is laced with landscaped grounds, and dotted here and there with the green expanses of golf courses. Pricey autos meander on the twisting roads and lanes, carefully avoiding vigorous young bicyclists and spandex-clad joggers who are seemingly everywhere.

What we are seeing in this direction is summit-grade American suburbia. On these sides of the school is an area where a massive influx of wealth has utterly transformed what was ranch land only 40 years ago, when Athenian was founded. Even houses in this area which aren't particularly grand sell for well over a million dollars. Newly developed "town homes" and condominiums which aren't far from the campus may be less prepossessing, but nevertheless fetch prices far beyond the reach of all but truly affluent families.

Athenian School was the brainchild of Dyke Brown and his wife Kate. As he ended a term as director of the prestigious Ford Foundation, Dyke Brown was determined to found a school in his native California which would "foster the continuing growth of each student across the entire range of his capacities…with the objective of helping him along the road towards becoming a mature and integrated human being." Calling on the advice of friends such as David Murray and on his own recollections of a single pre-war year spent as a student at an extraordinary boarding school in Germany, the Schüle Schloss Salem, Brown sketched out the idea of the school he wanted to create on a sheet of wrapping paper laid out on a table in the kitchen. On this paper a grand design emerged, of a school which would address "seven interrelated areas" of growth and learning — "understanding of self and others, bodily capabilities, spiritual capabilities, understanding of nature, understanding of society, understanding of MAN, [and] rational capability (in thought, words and symbols.)" The central part of the mandala-like design which the Browns created is made up of three concentric circles, each of which is divided into seven pie-shaped arc segments — one for each of the seven "understandings" the school would seek to foster in its students. Within segments of these pie-slices are specific explanations in relation to disciplines to be explored and pedagogies / activities to be employed.

In a corner of this sheet is Brown's gloss on a single key term — "understanding." It reads:

The word "understanding" is used here to encompass not only cognitive comprehension but also emotional and aesthetic evocation…the goal is to create a sense of wonder, awe and inspiration, in parallel with factual knowledge and intellectual grasp.

And faintly written in another corner, near sketches of what the circle-diagram might look like if it were seen in three dimensions, as a sort of cone, are three words:

Making
Knowing
Being

Clearly, Athenian School had already embarked on a deeply considered mission on the day it opened its doors in the rural country that lay well beyond the San Francisco sprawl.

Four decades have passed since then. When I spoke with Dyke Brown in the spring of 2005, in his apartment at a retirement center in Oakland, he was close to his ninetieth birthday. Kate had died several years before this time, and Dyke had retired as the Head of school at Athenian more than a quarter century earlier. Yet his enthusiasm for Athenian School remained that of a much younger man — his conversation about the school and the ideas which led to its formation were keen, energized, informed, and passionate. While he granted that, in 40 years, much had changed in and around the school, as it has in America, he nevertheless expressed a complete confidence that the aims and core direction of Athenian are "exactly the same" as they were when he launched the institution in the mid-1960's, and are as relevant now as they were then.

A group of young Athenian School teachers with whom I spoke vigorously agreed with this assessment. Yes, they said, "a 40-year mission" continues to be the keel under their school. As a result, "there is more humanity here." But they are frank in saying that "the mission is stressed" by the affluent consumer culture that has grown up around the school. This isn't a factor that is kept well beyond the school property, either; it comes into the school each and every day with those who learn and work there. Yet, the surrounding culture is a stress that is, so far, being confronted successfully, they believe. They point to "high student interest," "lots of enthusiasm," and an awareness among students and parents that "education out of classes really *does* matter." Such awareness doesn't come automatically, though —

nor does a realization among new faculty members that "we are teaching *kids* here, the Athenian way, and not just subjects." Staying on mission clearly is hard work.

A far more senior staff member talks about this mission / ambient-culture stress as a struggle which can only be won if the school will allow each of its students to "see another world" beyond the one he or she knows. This, he thinks, is regularly achieved through a process in which the school guides each student into new and instructive experiences through community service, international exchanges, and voluntary overseas service projects, participation in outdoor challenge, taking a responsible role in the government and maintenance of the school, and (to a growing extent) asserting environmental stewardship. He senses that, because these teenagers, like all those of their age, have "an insatiable appetite for the immediate," they tend to plunge with enthusiasm into these "experiential" activities. In fact, he says, the two "pinnacle experiences" at the school for most kids are not marked by athletic or academic triumphs, although Athenian's students excel in both ways. The "pinnacles" are the exchange / international service programs and the Athenian Wilderness Experience, a multi-day trek in California's Death Valley or in Yosemite Park, which has become a rite of passage for grade 11 students. "I used to see these programs as Athenian going into the world," says another older teacher. "Now I see it as the world coming into Athenian."

A group of graduates (from the 1970's through the late 1990's) concurs. What one sees at the school, they say, is "a philosophy made manifest." Education at Athenian, says another, provides "a compass for life…but not a roadmap." "Make sure it's clear in what you write," says another with great conviction, "that we are not talking about presenting kids with a *mold*. Rather, the school is opening up a *space into which a student can grow*."

Athenian is one of the schools which allies with St. Philip's to provide international exchanges and also to conduct international service projects during school vacation periods. These service programs aid people in need, and involve challenging physical work and rough living. Most are staffed by students from as many as a dozen countries. One young woman speaks of a specific moment during a service project in Ladakh, India. For days she had been coping with the stresses that come with hard, heavy work and high altitude, an unfamiliar country and culture, a wholly new peer group, privation, lack of anything like "normal" amenities and comforts, and direct contact with third-world poverty. "I was just *coping*," she says. "And then, one evening, at the end of a long, hard day, I sat down on a rock and looked out over that amazing landscape — and suddenly realized that I'd *adjusted*. And what came over me then was a sort of contentment. Contentment! It was the last thing I had ever expected to feel."

A graduate in his forties recalls going off for an exchange term to a school in northern Scotland. "The biggest challenge for me, really, was just in *going*. Leaving. Being there was all reward." He still regards it as "one of the largest life-changing experiences I've ever had."

For the Athenian students with whom I spoke, the school's international and service challenges are as much about discovering *themselves* as exploring the world and its people. Asked to rate the importance of the several priorities this school shares with its collaborators such as St. Philip's College, the Athenian kids overwhelmingly select the one that expects participating schools to "give the students opportunities for self-discovery."

Not all of the self-discoveries are painless, however valuable they may prove to be. A young alumna of Athenian wrote this account of what happened to her as the result of an exchange term she spent at a girls' school in England:

> *At the time, I was very focused on myself and had little patience for others, let alone an awareness of others' plights as teenagers. {But} being separated from my friends, my core unit, my support group, really awakened me to a different side of being a teenager. I was no longer in a stable position…and had to essentially "start over" if I were to gain a comfortable position like the one I had grown so used to at Athenian. I also had to choose whether or not to pursue that path.*
>
> *I chose not to, and spent my three months…reflecting on how my actions affected others, both there and {back at} Athenian. I came home to my dorm room in Danville a very different person, one who had learned that each and every student has something to share with others as well as unique talents that others could learn from, regardless of popularity or other symbols of social status.*

One of the pieces of advice I was offered by an Athenian student was to "focus on individuals." This story illustrates why that youngster's advice is valid. The primary ingredient in experiential education is always the individual *person* who is involved…with all the personal "baggage" he / she happens at that moment to be carrying. For the young woman who told me this story of her exchange term, the learning she achieved through exchange had little to do with the country she was visiting, and a great deal to do with the perspective she had gained on the price she had been paying for the way she had been living back in California, which until then had seemed "successful." Her term abroad turned out to offer her the discovery of what she had not until then known she needed: *compassion*.

Athenian's founding Head, who was one of the creators of this international collaboration between schools in the 1960's, would be delighted by this story. "The aim," Dyke Brown told me, "was to foster the basic qualities in human beings that induce concern for others and for society."

Eleanor Dase, the current Head of Athenian, adds that placing a student for an extended period in a different school setting, or as part of a multi-national team which does challenging service work together, day after day, is a critically important factor if this "fostering" is to succeed. "It is important for there to be genuine relationships," she says. Knowing what we do about adolescent development, that's a point of view that's hard to argue with.

In reminiscing about his own schooling and Athenian's driving purpose, Dyke Brown recalls how Kurt Hahn, then the Head of Schüle Schloss Salem, challenged students such as himself to think deeply about the parable of the Good Samaritan. "I realized that story was at the heart of his thinking," Brown tells me. What Brown does not go on to say, but the Athenian's graduate's story illustrates, is that the Good Samaritan story is really about how goodness actually reveals itself: *only* through action. Experiential education is aimed at revelations of just this kind.

"Making / Knowing / Being:" the words Brown wrote on his wrapping-paper plan for a new sort of American school, are beginning to explain themselves, aren't they?

§

The view from the campus of Starehe Boys' Centre and School, in Nairobi, Kenya, is far from scenic. While Kenya does have stunning vistas — seacoast, grasslands, lakes, the vast rift valley and high mountains — and while birds — black kites, vultures, the occasional Marabou stork — do fly overhead, what lies beyond Starehe's lovingly tended campus is a slum such as one finds only in the third world. Years of post-colonial corruption, the flight of countless people to the city from the countryside amid a general population explosion, and the steady economic marginalization of sub-Saharan Africa, have all shaped the desperate poverty of the Nairobi neighborhood which lies just beyond the school's gate.

What's within the gate on this November day is both a total contrast to the environment outside, and could not possibly be more deeply and purposefully connected to it.

The Starehe Boys' Centre and School (an identically fashioned but far newer Starehe Girls' Centre and School is located a few miles away) has its roots in a form of institutional evolution that has been no less ambitious than the one Dyke Brown conceived for Athenian School, but in the case of Starehe, was not generated according to a diagram drawn on a kitchen table. Starehe unfolded, year after year, though a perilous process of trial and error, based on the willingness of those who founded it to experiment, their determination to prevail, and an almost desperate wish to rescue boys who might otherwise have had no chance to amount to anything.

Starehe began amid the chaos of a bitter war. Three young Kenyans, Geoffrey Griffin, Geoffrey Geturo, and Joseph Gikubu, who were for decades not only the administrators but the driving forces behind Starehe, began their school as little more than a rescue effort, an attempt to save imperiled young people. The three men had resolved to find a way to take adolescent boys out of internment centers (effectively, concentration camps) where they had been imprisoned by the British Colonial Government during the "Mau Mau" insurrection. Some of the youngsters sent to their "boys' centre" from the camps proved to be too angry and uncontrolled to reach or rehabilitate. But in many cases, the youngsters who arrived were far from hopeless. Some had been jailed for little or no legal reason, without due process; a good many were guilty of nothing more than homelessness. However, with each day they were imprisoned along with adults who had been hardened by years of brutal warfare, their healthy development and potential worth as citizens was being destroyed.

The strategy which led to today's school began as a sort of structured re-socialization program. The founders experimented with a variety of approaches and programs intended to help boys learn the personal and social behaviors and basic skills they would need to become acceptable citizens in a free country. Again and again, the innovations which succeeded were those which involved the boys in learning how to become good citizens by *being* good citizens — through acting as responsible, effective, caring people within the small world of Starehe.

What they initially proposed to provide was "rehabilitation," but before long those both within the "Boys' Centre" and beyond it started to realize that a far more powerful transformation was taking place at Starehe. What, they began to imagine, could the same approach do for others, including those who were not so imperilled? Eventually they determined to reconstitute the "Boys' Centre" as a "Boys' Centre *and School*." The audacity of that step is well captured by the phrase that became the motto of Starehe when it was recognized as a school in 1966: *Natulenge Juu!* (Aim High!). Thus a rescue program aimed at rehabilitating imprisoned boys started a process that has led Starehe to become one of the African continent's great schools.

When I was at Starehe in late 2004, forty years had passed since the institution had transformed itself from a "Boys' Centre" to a "Boys' Centre and School." (The distinction originally was important, as the three men who founded and led Starehe had no experience or training as schoolmasters and, in fact, had none of the formal qualifications one would normally have needed just to obtain a basic teaching job — in effect, Starehe's later success and recognition as a school "certified" its leaders as educational administrators.) Starehe is now a famous school. Its graduates enter the world's most prestigious universities, even though to do so most of them must be given full financial aid. And with well over thirty applicants for every place in this 1,000-student school, admission to Starehe has become extraordinarily selective. Students come from every part of Kenya, and from every tribal and religious group.

But even now, Starehe primarily serves youngsters from disadvantaged backgrounds. In this school, the attainment of excellence has *not* invited elitism. No change in Starehe's admissions policy is contemplated. At least two-thirds of each year's intake of new students continues to be made up of youngsters from circumstances which are too impoverished to enable families to pay any fees at all. This practice has required a good deal of heroic fund-raising over the years, for even though life at Starehe is simple by western standards, and expenses are managed tightly, finding the money to pay for ambitious schooling in a poor country is a huge challenge. But the money has been found; and by now endowment gifts from successful graduates are beginning to relieve the frantic struggle to fund the school each year via grants from international charities and corporate sponsors.

Starehe's struggle to find a way to pay its bills notwithstanding, the school has become one of the greatest and most hopeful institutions in its country. As one Kenyan leader of national stature said to me a few years ago, "we only have to get through another few years here in Kenya. Then the Starehe boys will arrive."

Is there a better way to say that a school is *important*?

Geoffrey Griffin, the founding director of the school and, at the time of my visit, still very much its leader, was quick to admit that the international collaboration his school enjoys with schools such as St. Philip's and Athenian and scores of others brings benefits to Starehe that are different from those gained by some of the other schools in this group. Starehe, for instance, needs no encouragement in regard to a service commitment. It has long asked all students to take part in active social-service work through its voluntary service program. This has proved to be a strong antidote to the sort of entitlement and arrogance which a first-rate education might otherwise provoke among students in a country like Kenya, where even an adequate education is a rare commodity.

The school may also be the most thoroughly democratic school one could find. In a great many ways, students actually *run* the school at Starehe, through an elaborately-layered, consensually-developed student leadership structure. Starehe's is a culture which expects order, self-discipline, and tolerance. It has from the beginning combated tribalism and religious bigotry, in part by putting a high and explicit value on kindness and caring (the students have long referred to each other as "brothers"). It is also an institution where, even when they aren't in charge, the boys usually know they are valued contributors to decision making, and they are unafraid about speaking up.

An example of this democratizing process can be seen in one of the most important weekly events at Starehe — the *Baraza*. Reminiscent of a New England town meeting, the Baraza is actually derived from a traditional Kenyan community gathering. Starehe's weekly Baraza includes all students, student leaders, and administrators. It is an occasion when anyone in the community may ask anything of anyone else, respectfully, but with a guarantee that there will be no negative consequences after the Baraza — and expect to get a straight, honest, respectful answer. Some time ago Griffin wrote out a transcript of a typical Baraza interchange:

> Boy: *A prefect caught me playing about during a meal and wrote my name in his book. Then he forgot about me. Then, after three weeks, he read his book and remembered. So now he has put me on working party. I don't think it is fair to keep me waiting so long for my punishment.*
> Griffin: *Does the prefect want to comment?*
> Prefect: *It was me, sir. It's true I forgot; but I don't see why he*

should get away with it.
Griffin: *Although the rules say nothing about it, I think everyone accepts that punishment...shouldn't be delayed too long. In my own case, if I can't deal with a boy in a reasonably short time, I will let him go free...I think you should do the same. A limitation of about a week might be reasonable. (Loud applause.)*
Griffin *(noticing a hand with two fingers raised, indicating the owner's wish to make a supplementary comment):* {*The School Captain*} *wishes to say something.*
School Captain *{leader of the senior prefects' council — the school's most prominent student leader}: They are making a lot of noise because they think they can now duck punishments by spinning out the time before they do them. I don't think this is what you meant, sir?*
Griffin: *No, of course not. The limitation only applies if the delay is the fault of the prefect. Not if it is the fault of the boy.*
Boy: *Anyway, may I be let off my working party?*
Griffin: *Sorry, not by me. The prefect is within his rights since he punished you before this new ruling was made. He can forgive you himself if he wants to. Go and talk to him after Baraza.*

Starehe's Baraza is part parliament, part family get-together, and part teaching-about-citizenship-and-leadership-on-the-fly. It carries enormous importance for students. At a Baraza I attended, shortly before the end of a school year, several boys who were in their final weeks of school stood up to say something which in fact had little or no substance, and in a couple of cases ended in mid-sentence. They were just doing this so that a friend could take a picture of them in the act of speaking at a Starehe Baraza. Doing this was understood by all as a fond "rite of passage" — and the interruptions were cheerfully indulged.

What the connection with other schools around the world brings to Starehe is an international perspective that this very "national" school (only Kenyans attend Starehe) which is located in a third-world city would otherwise lack completely. The Director saw this as a matter of great importance for his school's students, not just to help potential leaders of Kenya gain a world context, but as a way of shaping what their hopes for their *own* country really ought to be. For this reason, the association matters deeply to Starehe. As a result of its connection with schools like St. Philip's and

Athenian, students exchange to and from Starehe, and many more come each year from partner schools all over the world to join Starehe boys (and now girls) in rural service projects during vacation periods.

In conversation with Starehe's students, the words I heard most often in describing the school's international connections were "service" and "self-discovery." Often the words occurred in the same sentence. But there were also individual stories to tell, and some of these were very powerful. One young man wrote to me about being part of an international project in Kenya:

> {We were}...to build a school for mentally and physically handicapped children. Thanks to the project, more than 50 disabled children, who had hitherto been kept in isolation — shunned by both society and their own families — would now be able to access elementary education and formal treatment. Even though the building was the main objective, reflecting back on it now I realize that it was a symbolic act...a show of the amount of good that can be done in a small amount of time when people come together and work towards a common goal. {And} the project brought together students from nine countries.

He also described how, at the end of an international event of this kind, it "...has never ceased to [amaze] me to watch people who have only known each other for a [short time] weeping as they say goodbye to each other." This, for him, points to their shared discovery of what he sees as the deepest lesson taught by such experiences: *universal human worth.* "Every person is just as important as the next one."

The impact is no less for students who visit Starehe. A graduate of Athenian recalls taking part in a "tree planting" at Starehe. "At the time I did not realize the significance or true importance of the planting of a tree, but in hindsight, I feel very fortunate to have been a part of that experience...it showed me how all of my actions (big and small) affect the world [and] reaffirmed the belief that I have the ability to *really* make a difference."

Most service work done by these international groups is humble, of real local value, and physically hard. A Starehe student recalls how, on an international project, all the participating students spent days "engaged in ...ferrying stones from one point to another. I realized then that one person's failure to fully participate in this kind of take-and-pass-on work [would make it] impossible for the whole project to succeed...[In much the same way] in the world, for anything to succeed completely, it will need support from *all* of the world. Laxity of some people might cause the failure of the whole scheme."

These remarks illustrate the kind of larger impact Starehe's links to schools beyond its locality and its continent can have for all involved. But it may also be worth marking these two stories for later reference, so as to be able to consider them again when we assess how education at a Round Square school actually works.

One more anecdote from Starehe: for many years, one of the most common kinds of voluntary service provided by Starehe students has caused them to be messengers, clerks and orderlies in clinics and hospitals. One boy related how, in the course of working as an orderly in a rural hospital, he

> *for the first time came across an AIDS patient. I was terrified to the bone, but there he was, waiting for a word of encouragement...so I had to make a decision. And from that day on, I learnt to live with him like he was normal. What I really learnt was how AIDS patients are segregated, and how they feel; and I also learnt that I would never do this sort of thing to them.*

§

I've just sketched brief vignettes of three schools in three different parts of the world. Each is, in a variety of ways, strikingly unlike the others. But while each may also be just as much unlike five dozen other schools which are part of the worldwide working partnership called Round Square, there are common characteristics in this global group.

First, all are schools which to a considerable degree are independent of higher-order administration. All are able to set their own, localized goals, and to design their own programs. If we can resist the temptation to pigeon-hole them for the most part as "independent" or "private" or "public" or "self-governing" schools (terms which mean, and even more importantly, connote, vastly different things in different countries), what we will find is that, regardless of matters such as funding sources, religious affiliation, socio-economic and cultural factors, school size and gender basis, and also regardless of the degree to which some sort of national academic curriculum is imposed, all are governed in such a way as to enforce a high level of *accountability for the moral and ethical characters of individual students*, and the long-term social consequence of each of these youngsters.

Second, in their shared concern for nurturing and guiding the *person* who is in fact "the student," Round Square schools also share several common objectives in relation to educating each person. These are goals of *principle*, not statements suggesting an orthodoxy of practice or pedagogy. Most students in Round Square schools know these objectives by heart, and will recite them for the inquirer as *"The Ideals."*

Actually, "Ideals" is an acronym:

>International understanding
>Democracy
>Environmental stewardship
>Adventure
>Leadership
>Service to others

Each of these six concepts will be examined in detail later in this book. But suffice it to say for now that all are considered *educational matters of essential importance* by each of the participating schools, and all are in practical terms best learned through a young person's *actual, individual, hands-on, invested experience*.

Third, the schools also have shared circumstances in common. From the onset, these circumstances have caused the adults who have led and governed the schools to foresee a world where economic and social convergences won't be a choice; they will be a fact of life.

Presuming that they are correct, responsible schools must prepare young people to understand a changing and far less parochial world. It is no coincidence that all but one of Round Square's founding schools were from Germany and Britain, or that for a time Round Square was primarily made up of European schools. Yes, the Cold War was dividing the world at that time; but in Europe, the European Community was *also* being formed, and the survivors of two catastrophic twentieth-century wars felt a deep need to invent new, trans-national social structures which would make yet another European war unlikely. In much the same way, nations which had recently been colonies of the "great powers" were at first disinclined to partner with schools in what had been the dominant nations. But when globalization began to "flatten" the world, the implications for schools in *all* nations became obvious, and post-colonial reluctance seemed to become less important.

Fourth, the leaders of each of the schools realized that, standing alone, their own school could at best provide an educational experience which was incomplete, isolating, and potentially misleading to students. St. Philip's has the "down-side" of frontier life and frontier values in "Alice" to contend with. Athenian knows all too well the nature of the challenge to the school's purpose which is posed by the affluence of its immediate environment. Starehe, too, needs to help students see life from a wider point of view than that which comes into the school with the students and which lies just beyond its gates. Only if it presents a *global* perspective can Starehe's students realize just *how high* their "aim" should really be.

Much the same can be said for, and by, all Round Square schools. Their situations are as different as Cape Town, South Africa, is from Hinterzarten, Germany, or Lima, Peru, is from Dehra Dun, India. But the essential insight is exactly the same. To truly succeed, each school must help students reach resources of perspective which can *only* be generated by experiences which lie well beyond the school itself, and often beyond the nation in which the school is located.

Finally, the growing understanding of how young people actually develop and learn has been gradually leading thoughtful people in the general direction of something like Round Square for the better part of a century. When school leaders are relatively unconstrained by higher-level bureaucracy, and are also free of the professional and political *idées fixes* which might limit more conventionally focused educators — in other words, when "thinking outside the box" doesn't require a huge leap from one's ordinary way of thought — then wholly new notions of what is possible and desirable can occur.

Thus it was that a confluence of ideas emanating from the social sciences began to link with practical knowledge of how to lead young people — knowledge which often had been acquired not through schoolmastering, but from business management, military service, adventure camping, rehabilatory work, or scouting. When one reads through the histories of the collaborating schools, one often finds such "outside the box" leaders — innovative pragmatists, people whose imaginations had been captured by the potential and worth of each individual human being who was in their charge. The mottoes they developed for their schools are revealing. These statements often seem to be summoning the young not to obedience (the purpose of most school mottoes), but to *power*:

"*Plus est en vous*" (There's more in you than you think):
Gordonstoun School, Elgin, Scotland

"*Natulenge Juu*" (Aim High):
>Starehe Boys' Centre and School, Nairobi, Kenya

"*Be Worthy of Your Heritage*":
>Deerfield Academy, Deerfield, USA

"*We teach not for school but for life, we train not for time, but for eternity*":
>St. Cyprian's School, Cape Town, South Africa

What's the result? As will be my practice wherever possible in this book, I'll refer this question to one of the students, who will tell her story:

During the Deerfield Round Square Conference in 2004, I went on a hiking expedition with about 70 other delegates. I was one of the first five people to reach the summit. With me were a Peruvian boy, an Australian boy, a Kenyan boy, and another American girl.

We were all quite out of breath after quickly scaling the final rock-covered ascent to the summit, and we stood around in silence once we arrived. The Peruvian took out his camera, and without saying anything, we all must have felt that taking a {group} picture was the appropriate thing to do. Then we all turned and looked at the landscape surrounding the summit (supposedly one can see six states) and commented on nature's beauty. Next, we sat down and pulled lunches from our backpacks and began eating, mostly in silence.

I didn't feel like I had to speak to any of these people to communicate with them. If nobody had been able to speak English, it wouldn't have mattered. We had all climbed a mountain that belonged to none of us, we had looked onto a landscape that belonged to all of us, and the language with which we understood these things amongst each other was universal. The fact that there was such international diversity in a group of five people only intensified the purity of our common understanding of the words "nature," "beauty," "pride," and "teamwork."
>— Female student, USA

Chapter 2:
Round Square — the First Half Century

It is now more than fifty years since a group of teenagers and adults from three western European schools arrived on Cephalonia to assist in rebuilding a home for the elderly which had been destroyed in an earthquake. All thought this would be just "a school-vacation volunteer service experience" — no more, no less.

Let's allow those who were present to tell the story of what actually happened:

> *20th July 1954. Araxos aerodrome, Patras, Greece. The three {planes} of the Hellenic air force were late and our small group was waiting in the dark. It was very warm and the cicadas had stopped singing for the night. The silence was almost total, except for a few remarks of the reception officials. Then the distant drone of the approaching planes raised hectic activity to light the flare path, and a hundred tired students ... descended from the planes.*

The speaker is one of the two Heads of schools who were present — Jocelin Winthrop Young, then a youthful ex-Royal Navy officer who was at the time Headmaster of the Anavryta School, in Greece.

The other school Head arrived with the students: Prince George of Hanover, then Head of the Schüle Schloss Salem, in southwestern Germany. With him was a group of secondary school students who would otherwise have been on their summer holiday.

As we let Prince George describe the mission which brought him to this place, we should keep in mind that he and Winthrop Young came from nations which were less than ten years away from their second devastating war in a half-century:

> *In 1954 an international labour camp was organized by Salem {to re-build a home for old people} on the island of Cephalonia ...the idea was conceived...after the terrible earthquake in the Ionian Islands, when I saw the misery in which the {old} people there were living, without hope of getting a roof over their heads*

> *in the foreseeable future.*
>
> *Appeals were sent out to...schools in various parts of Europe. From the first it was emphasized that the work would be very hard and that only strong and healthy youngsters could be used for the job. Warning was given that the accommodation would be extremely primitive and the heat very great...*
>
> *The response to the appeal was astounding. By the time the first few replies had come from the schools which had been approached our quota had been far exceeded.*

That reaction from Europe's young people was merely the first of a great many surprises which flowed from the Cephalonia relief project of 1954. However, it is clear that before one youngster had stepped off the airplanes and before a shovel had been lifted or a wheelbarrow had been pushed by anyone in the group, the enthusiasm of the students, their altruism and willingness to take risks and endure hardship so as to give to others, and their readiness to step up and lead, had taken charge. Winthrop Young and Prince George may have been the "men in charge" of this project, but the students were from the first the force that was really driving it towards its goal.

Teachers who are good at their work occasionally have a chance to glimpse brief, magical moments when a task or an activity so captures students' imagination that everything about the undertaking seems to "take off." Suddenly, something much more than a "project" or schoolwork begins to happen. Energy flows in prodigious amounts; goals are raised; boredom and passivity vanish; and leaders emerge, often to their own surprise as well as the astonishment of others. Dissidents and nay-sayers mutate into active, positive role players. A transformed, powerful group begins to express itself. The "astonishment" of the project's organizers as this kind of event developed was the first indication that *something special* was going on. Even more remarkably, this "something special" would continue to develop, day after day, to everyone's continued astonishment.

Among the other adults who took part in this service project was Roy McComish, a young teacher from Gordonstoun School in Scotland. He soon found that he was not going to be present as a bystander:

> *We all worked very hard in the Greek August sun, backbreaking work...the Headmaster of Salem at the time, Prince George of Hanover, was in charge of the expedition (**he worked harder than anyone**). [emphasis mine.]*

Now, headmasters are normally exalted creatures. Even young teachers (as McComish was at that time) do not often break a sweat in the course of the usual kind of day. Here, though, one headmaster — I have met him, and he is not a compulsive pick-and-shovel toiler — had become so wrapped up in the spirit of what was happening in this hard undertaking that he was, like the students, plunging into the thick of the work. "In charge" he may have been, according to his own role; but who was *leading* whom was quite another thing.

Winthrop Young was often out of sight. McComish, as an inquisitive young teacher, presumed that, as befitted his rank, this grandee was probably "sipping cool drinks back in Athens." Not so. Only after the project ended "...did I discover what Jocelin had been up to. The logistics — the supplies for the whole operation — had been in his hands throughout that torrid eight weeks. We were extremely well fed...medical supplies — more necessary than expected — were always immediately forthcoming, and we were constantly supplied with essential building tools and materials for the work."

Winthrop Young, summoned just as Prince George had been by the spirit of an extraordinary moment, was also doing something seldom seen among senior educational leaders. He was in charge of things, but was doing so *invisibly*, humbly ceding the limelight to others, and performing flawlessly so that the students might have an experience which was proving to be transformative for them.

Prince George describes what then ensued:

> *Half {of the students} slept on the floor, the others in camp beds...it was arranged that the various nationalities should be mixed up together. {Due to the extreme mid-day heat} working hours were from 6 to 11 in the morning and from 4 to 7 in the afternoon. {The local people} at first had doubts whether we were really in a position to manage...but soon took us into their work community, lending us tools if anything was missing and giving a helping hand if somebody did not know how to proceed. {And the students} of various nationalities were silently united by their efforts.*
>
> *When we had not much time left, and it looked as though the home was not going to be finished, some {students} suggested working at night, in shifts. I made no attempt to force this...so many signed {up} that we were able to organize two*

> *night shifts — from 21-23.30 hours and from 23.30 to 02.00.* **We could not work any longer than this because the electric light was switched off.** [Emphasis mine.]

Only a power shut-off could now curb what was happening!

While Winthrop Young credits the success of the project to "the inspired leadership and example of Prince George," and while he sweepingly grants that "for all engaged in the enterprise it has remained a unique and fascinating experience," something especially remarkable was happening to — and through — *him*:

> *Although my responsibility was largely in Athens, dealing with the supplies and the authorities involved,* **I visited the site several times and was so impressed that I decided to try and create a permanent organization to deal with such emergencies.**

Was this the flash of insight that enabled an essential new educational idea to be glimpsed in the midst of what had until then only been a summer-vacation social-service project? Not really. The spark *was* there. The students who were in Greece that summer had created it. Their enthusiasm, their growth in and through the service experience, the way they repeatedly stepped forward to lead the project to success, and the way their commitment helped transcend the barriers of eight different nationalities and at least as many languages, had powerfully "impressed" Jocelin Winthrop Young.

But the vision which eventually became Round Square wasn't yet clear to him, or to anyone else. For as "impressed" as he was, Winthrop Young hadn't gotten the whole point. He saw the events of 1954 as illustrative of a need to create an *"organization to deal with...emergencies"* rather than one formed to develop and sustain, on an abiding basis, the kind of powerful educational experience he had seen happening to the students who were in Cephalonia. What was important wasn't what the young people were doing — disaster relief work — but *what the experience of providing this service was doing to them.*

Also, what had brought him and Prince George together as developers of the Cephalonia project — they had both been pupils of Kurt Hahn, one of the twentieth century's most creative and charismatic educational leaders — seems to have been as much in Winthrop Young's thought as what he had seen happening on that Greek island. No doubt this background had much to do with their readiness to trust each other and to have faith in the students' ability to carry out collaborative work successfully and selflessly. But while they shared a concept of education which each had literally learned at Hahn's knee, the personal source of their shared vision — Hahn — was also a constricting force.

In that same year, 1954, Hahn had been forced by illness and old age to retire. For Winthrop Young, twice a student of Hahn's, first at Salem and later as one of the first pupils at Gordonstoun, and profoundly affected by both schools, Hahn's departure from the educational scene provoked what would become a lifelong commitment to education. But what he was also feeling was a sense of duty to preserve and propagate Hahn's vision, and to ensure that Hahn's "legacy" would endure. In Winthrop Young's words:

> *The success of the {Greek} project coupled with Hahn's retiring led me to believe that co-operation between...schools was imperative if the principles and practice of the Founder were to survive. His dominating personality had carried the movement so far, but even he was not immortal.*

We are not talking about "emergency" service now, but rather about something quite different: a purposeful and enduring "cooperation between...schools."

However, what Winthrop Young had in mind *also* seems to have been aimed at memorializing "the Founder" [Winthrop Young's capital F!]. From the beginning, what was to become Round Square was expressing the conviction of an older generation that "the principles and practices" developed by Hahn must be preserved and propagated, and that a new organization of "Hahn schools" might achieve this objective.

It may be helpful at this time to comment briefly on Hahn, since his name will appear repeatedly in the upcoming pages, although (for reasons which will soon become obvious) it is not appropriate to the subject of this book to dwell on his particular life and career too extensively.

Kurt Hahn (1886 – 1974) was born in Germany to a well-to-do Jewish family, and was educated there and attended universities in both Germany and England. As World War I arrived, he returned to Germany and, though unfit for military service due to the after-effects of a nearly fatal sunstroke, he joined the civil government, ending up as the secretary to the Markgraf of Baden, who was the Kaiser's last Chancellor. The Markgraf, supported by Hahn, realized at an early date that Germany would lose the war, and that military efforts to change this situation, such as unlimited submarine warfare, would only lead to greater devastation, vast suffering, and a world embittered against their country. Unfortunately, their efforts to bring about an early and negotiated peace proved futile. By the time the war ended, both men left Berlin feeling that they had failed in the greatest challenge that would ever come their way.

In such a frame of mind, Hahn embarked on a trek in the Alps, where he ran across a group of student hikers from Abbotsholme School, in England. Their enthusiastic conversation about the unusual, inspiring school they attended began a process of thought and inquiry on Hahn's part which he soon shared with his friend, the Markgraf. The upshot was that the two decided to start a school on new principles, which might enable them to develop young people who would be able to lead responsibly, serve society with compassion, and see through the nationalistic enthusiasm which had blinded people of their own generation. Hahn would run the school; the Markgraf would be the Board Chair and would provide the school's home in the vast, largely vacant former Cistercian abbey which he owned in southwestern Germany, Schloss Salem.

Although postwar Germany was in near-anarchy, and few families had the resources to pay school fees, the new school was from the first a success. Before long Salem was sought out by thoughtful, imaginative parents and ambitious youngsters. The school was also, as Hahn had earnestly meant it to be, *different*. Students were challenged to take far greater responsibility for themselves, their school, and their community than was usually the case at that time, in Germany or anywhere else. Studies were not the only priority. Training for leadership, service to others, practical work, the arts, and adventure were all granted "curricular" value.

At some point during the 1920's, Hahn wrote out a list of seven "Laws of Salem" which were, in effect, marching orders for Salem's teachers and administrators:

> *Give the children opportunities for self-discovery.*
> *Make the children meet with triumph and defeat.*
> *Give the children the opportunity of self-effacement in the common cause.*
> *Provide periods of silence.*
> *Train the imagination.*
> *Make games important but not predominant.*
> *Free the children of the wealthy and powerful from the enervating sense of privilege.*

Students and teachers from other countries were welcomed at Salem. Thus from the beginning the Schüle Schloss Salem was able to present an "international" perspective. As the school ended its first decade, it clearly was on its way to great things.

The arrival of the Nazis changed all that. Because of its departures from "German" education and because it was led by a Jew, Salem was soon under increasing pressure. When Hahn began to clarify his opposition to the Hitler regime, and ultimately demanded that Salem graduates end their relationship with either Salem or the Nazi party, he was jailed. Urgent efforts to free him (these efforts included a plea from the British Prime Minister) resulted in Hahn's being allowed to escape from Germany in July 1933. Shortly thereafter he arrived in England without funds, employment, or what until then had been his profession.

But, with the aid of friends and colleagues, he soon rebounded. Less than a year later, Hahn opened Gordonstoun School in a nearly derelict great house near Elgin, Scotland, not far from Inverness. The school's early years were, in the words of one of the early and long-time staff members, "precarious" and a "struggle...for survival." Its progress was not aided by the British government's forced removal of the school to a wholly unsuitable location in Wales for much of World War II. Nevertheless, Gordonstoun did survive, returned after the war to its Scottish home, and then flourished.

Along the way, the Gordonstoun sea-training program became the model for Outward Bound. This movement has had an impact around the world. Another Hahn brainstorm, originally called "the County Badge Scheme," gained fame as the Duke of Edinburgh Award program (in some countries it is given other names, but the concept is the same). A final Hahn-conceived program of internationally-populated residential schools grew into the United World Colleges.

Hahn, both as an educator and innovator in service programs for youth, made a profound impact which reached far beyond the nations where he worked. As a former student said:

> *Hahn undoubtedly made an immense contribution to education in its broadest sense, and, inevitably, this makes him sound like some zealous reformer...in fact, of course, his heart was even bigger than his brain...eccentric perhaps, innovator certainly, great beyond doubt."* — HRH the Duke of Edinburgh

Unhappily, when the 1954 Greek project ended, time simply

passed. A meeting of the Heads of Salem, Gordonstoun and Anavryta in 1955, convened to explore the possibility of "ongoing collaboration," accomplished nothing.

"The failure was mine," Winthrop Young has said; but in fact it was a failure shared by all those who were present. While something wonderful had indeed happened during the 1954 service project in Greece, and while the Headmasters who met in 1955 shared a great deal philosophically, they had come to fear that their schools were "too far apart to enable consultation." As Winthrop Young later realized, they also lacked "a valid and detailed plan." In other words, they knew they had seen *something* which was profoundly exciting and worthy, and they suspected it might serve as a model for shared practice. But — in practical, detailed terms —how was this to be made to occur?

Most importantly, those who were present at the failed meeting of 1955 and at the various formal and informal conversations of school Heads which occurred in the years between 1955 and 1966 did not include the true energizers of the Cephalonia experience — the students. Indeed, it was not until students were once more powerfully and permanently returned to the center of the scene that what we now know as Round Square can truly be said to have emerged as an abiding institution.

How to make a central student presence integral to Round Square's identity was the most crucial and innovative part of the "valid and detailed plan" which Winthrop Young and his allies lacked in 1955, and which they labored in the ensuing years to develop. And it also mattered that taking such a leap — in the world of the 1950's and 60's, as the Cold War was settling in, when even small innovations in education seemed risky — would take will-power and courage, and — as it later turned out — a bit of a royal shove.

The spark that was lit in Cephalonia was *not* extinguished, however. It outlasted the adult leaders' failure to get something going immediately between their schools on a permanent basis. It endured despite the lack of funding for collaborative programs, and despite Hahn's apparent indifference. Efforts to initiate some sort of collaboration persisted. For example, in 1962, Winthrop Young received a generous grant from an American sponsor, Mrs. Lemon Clark, of Fayetteville, Arkansas, to travel to the U.S. in search of possible partner schools. While this trip resulted in a connection with a new school in California, Athenian, it failed to move the organization into being. In fact *eleven years* passed before the movement which was to be the result of the project in Greece finally came to life. That the spark persisted until the time for action was finally ripe is both astonishing and the best possible way to sum up how *powerful* — and ultimately, *defining* — that one-hundred-student service experience in 1954 had been.

In 1966, at an eightieth-birthday celebration for Hahn at Salem, in Germany, some of the same school leaders (Heads and governors) found time to meet again to discuss collaboration. On this occasion, however, two new factors were at hand. The first was, for many of those present, a heightened sense of duty towards Hahn, to whom many felt they owed so much. This sentiment is expressed in the "proposal" sent by Winthrop Young to eight schools' headmasters, all of whom had studied and / or worked with Hahn. This "proposal" served as the *de facto* agenda for the meeting. Dyke Brown, Head of Athenian, could not attend, but expressed an interest in ongoing participation; the Head of a second school declined the invitation. Hahn himself was absent, but all other Heads who were invited attended.

Winthrop Young's message read, in part, as follows:

> *Proposition:*
> *That there are now several schools in different countries, following the system originated by Dr. Hahn, between which there is little cooperation or exchange of information, although they are often faced by the same problems.*
>
> *Proposal:*
> *That on the occasion of Dr. Hahn's 80th birthday, a meeting of the Headmasters of the Schools present discuss the possibilities of setting up a "Salem Schools Conference" or "Hahn Schools Conference."*
> *That other schools working on similar systems deriving from those of Dr. Hahn, be invited to join.*

A second new factor was, for the first time, the presence at the meeting of a chairman who was *not* a school headmaster — the young King of Greece, a governor and graduate of Anavryta School, (and thus a former student of Winthrop Young's).

Perhaps King Constantine's youth was the crucial difference, or perhaps it was a universal disinclination of royal persons to put up with overlong discussions. Or it might just be that what was at work was a spirit which I have so often met in today's young Round Square students and graduates: *a readiness to act when action is needed.* In any case, those who were present recall his almost immediately asking the group of headmasters just one question: "is this something you believe should be done?" All agreed it was.

"Well then, *get on with it!"* he replied. And that was that.

The group set a date for an "organizing" meeting and agenda-setting roles were agreed upon. They elected Winthrop Young "Honorary Secretary" of the new group, and it was announced that the Old Salem (Graduates') Association was donating a prize in Hahn's name to the new organization. In barely twenty minutes, the session was over. The minutes barely run beyond a page. And Round Square was under way.

Or, more accurately — something that would *become* Round Square was under way. The mixture of motives that was present, as natural and important as this may have been for those involved, still had to be sorted out before the organization we now know as Round Square could develop and flourish. And oddly, it was only the firm determination of Hahn himself, at the very end of his life, *not* to let the organization which Winthrop Young and other Hahn admirers were creating become a Hahn memorial which stopped Round Square's founders from making it exactly that.

On February 28 and March 1, 1967, a small group of Heads and Governors met at Gordonstoun School, in a room in an ancient building called The Round Square, to found something they still intended to be the "Hahn Schools Conference." Those around the table were: Henry Brereton, Warden of Gordonstoun; Dyke Brown, Headmaster of Athenian; David Byatt, Headmaster of the Battisborough School; F.R.G. (Bobby) Chew, Headmaster of Gordonstoun; Kurt Hahn, Founding Head of Salem and Gordonstoun; H. Lessing, Governor of Salem; HRH Prince Max of Baden, Patron of Salem; Mrs. G. McClelland, Governor of Box Hill School; Roy McComish, Headmaster of Box Hill School; J.W. Stork, Governor of Battisborough; Capt. Ian Tennant, Governor of Gordonstoun; Capt. Tsoukalas, Headmaster of Anavryta; and Jocelin Winthrop Young, from Salem.

The minutes of that meeting make fascinating reading. No sooner had the group sat down and been welcomed than Hahn spoke up:

> *Dr. Hahn strongly pressed for a change in the name of the Conference. A discussion followed, and it was decided to rename the Conference "The 1966 Schools Conference."*

The other important items of business were that Aiglon College in Switzerland was invited to join the group, and that Brereton, Chew and Hahn were asked to draft a "statement...of aims and purposes."

The name that had been chosen, of course, was far less than ideal. "Absurd" might be a more apt description. No one who has spoken with me believes it was in fact a serious proposal; rather, the name was a "place card" meant to mark where the *real* name would go, when Kurt Hahn relented. However, as the hours and then a day passed and other items (publications, annual dues, notice boards, flags) had all been duly discussed, it became clear that Hahn was not about to change his mind. He was, as Byatt has recalled, "more emphatic" in his view of this question than many realized.

Eventually, at the third and final session, Prince Max said what all were thinking, that the "1966 Schools" idea was "...not satisfactory." As the minutes show, "...after a lengthy discussion, it was decided to rename the Conference 'the Round Square Conference.'"

Formal minutes, of course, elide much of what is most dynamic and interesting in any group process; but all those who were present and with whom I have spoken recall that the actual proposer of the new name was the person who had most urgently wanted to memorialize Hahn, Jocelin Winthrop Young.

Young later confirmed this. In a talk to those attending the 1974 Round Square Conference at Cobham Hall School, in England, he recalled:

> *We sat grimly in the Warden's Room at Gordonstoun and I looked out of the window at the curving walls of the old stable block: "What about Round Square Conference, nobody could read significance into that?" I suggested flippantly. And so it has remained, though from time to time members protest.*

By now, even those who were present at the formation of Round Square will grant that Hahn's refusal to lend his name to the project which would became Round Square was a generous decision, and beyond that, a wise one. However, even now, a half century later, when Winthrop Young returns to this moment in conversation, it is still possible to hear a hint of regret in his voice, although at the same moment he recalls that "I was very relieved to get off the leash and to move ahead with the adventure."

Hahn's stubborn determination freed Round Square at its very start from what would inevitably have been a distracting, restrictive self-definition. The elimination of the "Hahn" name did much to open the way for

Round Square's eventual spread around the world, to schools and nations where Hahn was of little influence or in fact was entirely unknown, but where similarly motivated institutions had emerged, under the leadership or influence of other visionary educators — Darling in Australia, Boyden in the U.S.A., Mackenzie in Canada, or Griffin in Kenya, for example.

These "non-Hahn" schools, which now are both a majority and among the most committed in the Round Square group, evolved similar ideas and principles on their own, to meet locally developing needs. Of course, the extent to which like-minded innovators may have inhaled the same intellectual / philosophical "air" during the late-nineteenth and early twentieth centuries is open to speculation. I will look more closely at this subject later in this book.

What is perhaps most important about Round Square's early history, though, is that its liberation from using Hahn as a pedagogical template seems to have released the organization from any tendency to develop an orthodoxy of method. Around the world, there has long been a tendency for creative educational ideas to swiftly become ossified into pedagogical dogma. *That didn't happen to Round Square.* Freed by Hahn from the impulse to promote a specific model of practice, Round Square and its member schools have been able to unite through a commitment to *shared ideals and objectives*, as expressed in common principles and priorities, rather than attempting to replicate a single methodology.

Clearly, the 1954 summer experience in Greece — even when the mixed motives and later false starts of those who witnessed it are reckoned with — was Round Square's starting point. A spark had been lit by the students in Cephalonia. The readiness of a handful of adults, all of whom had in one or more ways been influenced by Hahn, to *understand the value and importance of what they were observing*, and later to turn the spark provided by the students into flame, was Kurt Hahn's most important contribution to Round Square. The ability of Winthrop Young, Prince George, Roy McComish, and others to respect what the students were achieving and to sense its potential as an educational model meant that, once the participants in the 1954 project had created this spark, it was unlikely to go out.

During the months following the February / March meeting at Gordonstoun, Brereton (apparently alone) drafted what would become the first Round Square manifesto, the "statement of aims and purposes" which he had been asked at the Salem meeting to prepare as part of a committee of three. It is, as educational statements go, remarkably clear and succinct:

Round Square Conference

> *Membership of the Round Square Conference implies that the Headmaster or Headmistress of a member school recognizes and seeks to implement the following aims:*
>
> *Education should be concerned with the development of the whole man or woman in the pursuit of truth. It should employ a wide range of activities in the training of the mind and person. These activities should encourage self-realization, self-discipline, self-confidence, and the development of the imagination, the pursuit of academic excellence and positive health.*
>
> *Whilst the young should be encouraged to develop their particular gifts to the full, they must be prepared to sacrifice a measure of freedom and self interest to the community.*
>
> *The young should be given special responsibilities of a demanding nature in recognition of the fact that the school is a partnership between adults and young people in which mutual trust and understanding play an important part and in which active participation and involvement should be encouraged. Responsibilities should be graded according to maturity.*
>
> *Importance is attached to providing opportunities for the young to serve others both inside and outside the school.*
>
> *Education should present a series of graded challenges, physical, mental and moral, and the young should be taught to face failure as well as success.*
>
> *Every effort should be made to promote the mixing of boys and girls with dissimilar backgrounds as regards ability, religion, nationality and social background.*
>
> *Whilst the Round Square Conference is an association of schools in different countries which encourages co-operation across national frontiers, each school acknowledges local allegiance.*
>
> *The Conference was originally formed to cement the informal links that existed between the schools that had drawn their inspiration from Dr. Kurt Hahn.*

Brereton's draft was circulated, although not until a few days after an "interim" meeting of a smaller group of Heads had been held at Box Hill School in October of 1967. His draft was subsequently revised at the full

Conference meeting at Box Hill School on June 11th - 13th, 1968. While it is recorded that Brereton had written the re-draft following the meeting, the minutes record that there was "discussion of each paragraph" and that Brereton was asked to "re-draft, incorporating the alterations agreed upon, at his discretion where the exact wording was not finalised, and [that] this should be circulated." These words leave no doubt that the revised text was in fact a consensual product, and predictably, more wordy.

It is fascinating to examine where the nips and tucks and expansions were made in moving from the first draft (much of its vocabulary was preserved) to the second as Round Square became a more democratic organization — and in doing so, began to reveal the abiding direction in which *all* of those present (who now included a small number of students) intended to proceed:

Round Square Conference

It was agreed at the meeting of the Conference held in Box Hill on June 13th 1968 that the associated schools have the following aims in common:

They are concerned with the "whole man or woman," and regard as educationally relevant a wide range of human activities which they seek to include in the school programme or deliberately to encourage outside it. This is not to be taken to imply that they are less concerned with the training of the mind than other schools, rather the reverse. But they recognize that intellectual quality is itself furthered by disciplines and self confidence learnt in other fields, by a basis of positive health, and by an imagination well exercised in fields of practical enterprise and in the arts.

They recognize the need to train the young on the one hand to develop their particular gifts as individuals to the full and on the other to be willing to sacrifice a measure of freedom and self interest on behalf of the community. They look upon these two aspects of training, which must sometimes seem to conflict, as being nevertheless inter-dependent. "The good life is dependent on the good state."

They believe that the structure of the school community should depend to a large extent upon pupils themselves so that it would in a visible way break down if there was any general failure to respond to the various graded responsibilities. This is not to imply that the pupils can run the school; their responsibilities will be only part of a framework which must in essential sections be held together by adults. There is always the aim of partnership between adults and senior pupils and between seniors and juniors. Therefore there is also the aim to develop a basis of mutual respect and trust in all parts of the school. To this end self-discipline is regarded as a more worthwhile control than imposed discipline. Both however have their function in all the schools, and the results of these disciplines must be clearly discernible even if their operation is not conspicuous.

Important emphasis is placed upon training for service and it is suggested that service to the less fortunate is an obligation all should be trained to offer with competence. While the founder schools in the Conference accepted Christian teaching as basic to their aims — and this idea of service could scarcely have reached such dominant importance in the education without that teaching — yet the acceptance of the obligation to educate for service, rather than the profession of a particular religion, will be the basis for membership.

Schools generally have to be a compromise between educational ideals and what is financially practicable. The latter should not kill the purpose of enabling boys and girls to experience the enrichment of sharing their lives in school with others from dissimilar backgrounds. Familiarity with a wide range of human circumstance, during the years when attitudes are flexible but hardening is felt to be of first importance in 20th century education.

Whilst the Round Square Conference is an association of schools in different countries which encourages co-operation across national frontiers, each school acknowledges local allegiance.

What immediately strikes the eye is that this is a far more complex, convoluted text than the statement Brereton originally provided. It is more cautious, too, littered with statements such as "this is not to be taken as" and "this is not to imply that." It is also less hortatory — one hears less of "should be" — and more statements of fact — something "is" and certain other things "are." And the final reference to Hahn, which certainly was (given his prior objections) not what he would have wanted to see in such a document, was dropped. Hahn attended the Box Hill meeting, but whether this deletion was made at his specific request is not recorded.

However, the revised statement, even if its presentation is less bold, remains a profoundly radical one, not only for its era, but even for ours. The concept of curriculum, and by that measure, of education itself (here, "programme") is far broader than would commonly have been the case. The relationship of intellectual / cognitive learning to the far more expansive "whole man / whole woman" sense of educational purpose is made explicit and, in fact, is wholly integrated with it. The tension that exists in every school between the betterment of the individual and the need of the community isn't just admitted; it is *embraced*. Similarly, the role of discipline (both of the "self" — and "other" — varieties) is faced squarely. The first is declared preferable, but both are needed, and the sum of the two must be evident.

Service is retained as a goal of "important emphasis." However, this is followed by a rather abstruse bit of discussion concerning the relationship of service to Christianity (it is not hard to imagine how such an addition came to happen, or why the same text vanished from subsequent iterations of Round Square's "aims"). Remarkably, for a time when many schools had no financial aid programs at all, and many of the aid programs which existed were actually driven by a wish to attract top academic or athletic prospects, rather than to attain "diversity," this document commits member schools to providing aid so as to be *socio-economically* inclusive. Finally, the document preserves Brereton's original statement concerning national allegiances, which certainly grew out of the politics of the time. This pronouncement, too, has vanished in recent years, though nearly all of Round Square's member schools continue to be predominantly "national" rather than "international" in student population.

Perhaps because this pronouncement was such a departure from the norm, and almost certainly because of other developments in the world, including growing student unrest in schools and colleges, the expansion of Round Square over the next half-dozen years was slow. At the time of the Conference / Annual General Meeting at Gordonstoun, in 1973, there were nine member schools, all but two of them in Europe.

A lack of funding continued to be a problem. But the lingering question of whether Round Square was to be a "Hahn Club" was also a limiting factor. There is evidence that, despite Hahn's efforts, the "Hahn schools" issue was still incompletely resolved as late as 1973. In that year, still another effort was made by a member Head to amend the revised Brereton statement of "aims" to indicate that "the Headmaster or Headmistress of a member school recognizes the aims which are implicit in the philosophy of Dr. Hahn the founder of Salem and Gordonstoun and the architect of the Outward Bound Movement." No action was taken on this proposal, but the Hahn / non-Hahn issue continued to arise from time to time, even though it was increasingly seen by representatives of member schools as an expression of earnest, but rather digressive, sentiment. And even then the question was not completely put to rest. As late as 2000, a retired Head delivered an open letter to the Round Square Board which claimed that there was much to regret in the ongoing nature of the organization, and in particular stated that, among students at Round Square schools, "the absence of any real knowledge of Kurt Hahn or his place in 20th Century and probably 21st Century education is to be deplored." The letter was read with a mixture of professional courtesy and personal fondness for the writer, but brought no change in direction.

In plain fact, while Hahn had refused to lend his name to Round Square, he was not uninvolved. He simply had made a canny choice about how his involvement was to occur, and how it was to be perceived.

For a few years prior to his death in 1974, Hahn occasionally attended and, at times, spoke at Round Square events. The last statement occurred during a discussion of "the present student revolt" in universities in Europe, which was also developing in America. Hahn offered this perspective:

> *We must realize that one of the greatest difficulties is the spiritual gulf between the generations, a gulf that starts in the home. We must go deeply into the causes. The young are concerned about unnecessary misery in the world — the young of the U.S.A., France, Germany, and {Britain}. The curse of Hiroshima festers in the mind of the young. Vietnam protests, etc., are understandable reactions. {The older generation} does not bother enough about these miseries.*
>
> *The young are interested in world problems. But their revolutionary energies are deteriorating. One of the temptations {they face} today is moral indignation, which can escalate into a fight against authority which can become ruthless...and the tomatoes can become stones, and this can lead to murder.*
>
> *The older generation must embrace these causes to bridge the gulf with the young.*

Reading these extraordinary words, it is easy to imagine why Hahn had such a deep, lasting impact on the educators who worked with him!

The main event of each year for the newly formed Round Square community was an annual Conference, hosted by a member school. (Some years later, due to persistent confusion about whether one was referring to an organization or a meeting when one used the term "Round Square Conference," the organization's name simply became "Round Square." The term "Conference" is now reserved for the annual meeting.) During these early years, both the meeting and the organization itself were seen as an expression of the Heads of the member schools. Although students and staff members, as well as governors, had been attending the Conferences in small numbers since 1968, it was not until 1974, at the time of the Conference at Cobham Hall School, when the annual meeting began to evolve toward its present format. Thereafter it would be attended by school delegations which were required to include four constituencies (heads, governors, staff, students). The change in Conference representation was duly followed by steps taken in the late 1980's to clarify that the school, not the Head, is the Round Square member; and a bit later, to mandate that every school's delegation to the Conference must always have students as a *majority*.

The word most often used to describe the purpose of the annual Conference in Round Square's early years was "consultation." That is, the Conference was a way for schools to share ideas and report on what they were doing. It was to be a sort of "market place" where they could discuss needs, identify opportunities, and develop joint undertakings.

Sharing and reporting did indeed take place. Good ideas began to "leak" from school to school. And membership was at last expanding beyond Europe and America. In 1973, a school in Australia, The Southport School, from Queensland, joined Round Square. Its Headmaster, John Day, who had come to know about Round Square through Gordonstoun School, became an early and vigorous advocate for Round Square in Australia. In 1978, Lakefield College School, in Ontario, Canada, became the first Canadian member. Terry Guest, then Lakefield's Headmaster, soon was a tireless proponent of Round Square in North America, and later served as Round Square's Executive Director. But the general hope to see more multi-school service collaborations involving students, such as the 1954 undertaking in Greece, remained, for the most part, more a source of frustration than of pride.

Winthrop Young summed up the obstacles: "...difficulty in getting parental cooperation...academic stress and lack of opportunity...[it is]

almost impossible to find time and the chance to present the students with the necessary challenge." But then, ever eager to preserve the Kurt Hahn legacy, he turned to Hahn's summary of how the "sickness of modern western civilization" was affecting young people:

The decline of fitness...
The decline of memory and imagination...
The decline of skill and care, due to the weakened tradition of craftsmanship
The decline of compassion, due to the unseemly haste with which modern life is conducted
The decline of adventure and enterprise.

All these problems, he knew, could be confronted through a serious program of voluntary service which would unite students from many nations and cultures. *Yet this was simply not happening on a regular basis.* Several years passed before the problem which had been described by Winthrop Young was truly solved. During that interval, the individual schools were doing good work by way of service undertakings. One example which was eventually copied by several schools was "Gingerbread," a school-based summer camp for impoverished children developed in the 1970's by Windermere St. Anne's School. And the 1954 model of *ad hoc* relief efforts was not forgotten entirely. For instance, a multi-school "clean-up" project which involved students from several schools followed the Amoco Cadiz oil spill in 1977.

It was not until 1980, however, and the creation of the Round Square International Service (RSIS), a permanent, staffed resource for planning and supporting joint service undertakings for the students at all member schools, that a real solution emerged. Those who developed RSIS and led its first projects, in India, were a courageous band: Roy McComish; John Kempe, then Head of Gordonstoun; Gulab Ramchandani, Head of Doon School; and Shomie Das, of Lawrence School, Sanawar; Brian Jones, of Lakefield College School; and Ann West, then the Deputy Head at Cobham Hall and thereafter the Coordinator of RSIS. With them, just as essentially, were scores of pioneering students.

One of the first discoveries made by RSIS was that the model of providing "disaster relief" which was predicated on the 1954 project was inappropriate to the educational need they were trying to address. But it was only after a profoundly difficult and only half-successful first "pilot" international project in India in 1980, followed by McComish's utterly frank assessment, that this understanding was reached.

As Ann West recently recalled, the 1980 project, which was aimed at performing flood relief in southeastern India, ultimately had more to do with endless bus trips, needless discomfort, minor illnesses (which warned of greater risks), and bureaucratic entanglements. However, this "pilot" project, with its follow-up assessment, helped to clarify that the *student experience of service need not be based on a response to a disaster* or sudden crisis. It was only necessary that such projects *respond meaningfully to real need*. And many human needs — even desperate ones — abide throughout the world, rather than arriving without warning as do floods and earthquakes. Were Round Square to focus its service programs on meeting critical but abiding needs, that would admit the possibility of thorough advance planning, careful selection and training of leaders and participants, timing which would take advantage of the most economic travel options and fit comfortably into school calendars, and a routine which would enable RSIS to provide thoroughly developed logistics. In the third world context, particularly, but also in impoverished areas of the first world, such steps are essential to the conduct of service projects which will be safe, secure, and successful for those taking part as well as for those being served. This key insight, which was made possible by the 1980 "pilot," effectively opened the door to what is now an honored, adventurous, and routinely successful aspect of Round Square's world-wide programming.

In 1981, in no small part due to the involvement of staff and students in supporting the 1980 RSIS experiment, Doon School in Dehra Dun, India, became the first Indian member of Round Square. Round Square was thus present in Australia, Britain, Canada, Germany, India, Switzerland, and the United States. But a crisis — in retrospect, an entirely predictable, and ultimately a joyful one — was arriving.

In early 1983, Terry Guest, then Head at Lakefield, and Steve Davenport, Head at Athenian, (these schools were at that time two of the three Round Square members in North America), made a presentation about Round Square to Heads and staff members of U.S. and Canadian schools during a meeting of the National Association of Independent Schools (NAIS). Merely intending to report to colleagues on what they were doing, they presumed there would be limited interest in this international, experientially-oriented organization. To their astonishment, though, the meeting room was packed. And to their greater amazement, dozens of school leaders lingered after the presentation to express an interest in joining Round Square.

To assess whether this enthusiastic reaction was to be taken seriously, Winthrop Young announced a follow-up meeting to occur at an almost impossibly remote location (the Okanela Ranch, deep in the Colorado mountains) and at a terrible time of year for school leaders and senior staff (September, when schools in North America are just opening). Nevertheless, representatives of thirteen schools attended. Most expressed a determined interest in seeking Round Square membership.

This response in North America sent a shock wave through the Heads of the existing Round Square schools, who, as McComish later recalled, saw this development as inviting an "overloading of North American schools...which would have produced an imbalance." (Imbalance? What then, the North Americans wondered, might be seen as constituting "balance?") This apprehensive reaction of the part of the leaders of the existing Round Square member schools did not sit at all well with the Americans and Canadians. At a heated meeting with Winthrop Young in New York in early 1984, David Cruickshank, then Head of Bishop's College School in Québec, Canada, spoke for all when he termed Round Square's response "Eurocentric." While this accusation was not entirely fair, it was a charge which came too close to the mark for comfort.

Meanwhile, the North Americans, impatient to make something happen, set up their own version of Round Square, a regional collaboration, which they called the "Okanela Conference." Almost instantly exchanges began happening between these schools, and a series of superb summer service projects in northern Canada and western Montana were developed. Before long, the intended point had been made. These schools were in all but the formal ways "Round Square institutions." Over the next few years, many Okanela schools became Round Square members (there are at this writing 14 member schools in North America). The "Okanela Conference" acknowledged the end of the standoff over expansion of Round Square membership by quietly vanishing at the end of the 1980's.

Just as Round Square, thanks to the North American invasion (quickly followed by waves of Australians, Indians, and Africans) was becoming "non-anything-centric," so too was it being forced to evolve in formal and institutional ways. In 1987 the locus of membership devolved from the Head to the School. The hitherto rather casual governance process via a "Council" dominated by Heads in Britain and Continental Europe evolved in the early 1990's into a true Board of Governors, many of whom were *not* school Heads. At the same time, the crucial role of staff leaders of Round Square programs at member schools (customarily called "RS Reps") was recognized, first by supporting improved networking for these leaders, and secondly by inviting the Reps annually to elect a member of their group to sit on the Board. The immediate consequence of these steps was a significant increase in the number of student exchanges and the recruitment of more junior staff members to participate in RSIS projects.

During the early and middle 1990's, the Round Square Board undertook its first-ever strategic planning process. This endeavor was also the first major piece of work which Round Square's leadership primarily conducted using the Internet. A major result was creation and funding of a full-time position of Executive Director, to be assisted by the RSIS Director, and supported by appropriate business / clerical staff. Terry Guest, the former Head of three Canadian Round Square member schools (Lakefield, Sedbergh School, and Bayview Glen) was appointed to the new position.

§

A half century after the summer work project in Greece, what had been a small, European-centered network of cooperating schools had metamorphosed into something that was beginning to look global. Round Square has also been repeatedly transformed along the way.

In size alone, Round Square has grown dramatically. No longer Eurocentric nor tiny, it is truly worldwide. It includes over 60 full-member schools, more than 15 regional affiliates, and a cluster of applicant schools. There are Round Square schools on every continent and in eighteen nations. Growth continues, with the most rapid advances at this time occurring in Australasia, Southwest Asia, the Americas, and Africa.

Every year both Round Square and its member schools send teams of students on voluntary service projects to every continent. Each of these projects is, in a way, a direct descendant of the 1954 project in Greece. However, for each student who is involved, the projects are a wholly new and unprecedented experience — and are often described by them as "life-changing." (Of course, they are *meant* to be just that!)

Round Square's annual student / adult Conference, which functions as a kind of combined camp-meeting, seminar, and parliament, now brings together over 500 delegates (more than half of whom must be students) from around the world. Delegates assemble at one or more host schools for a week — to assess and plan projects, activities, and exchanges for the coming year, discuss a selected world challenge in depth, and hear how this topic and the world looks to colleagues from other countries and cultures. They also hear from peers about service projects or expeditions which have taken place, and consider these reports as models for possible undertakings of their own. The delegates develop sustainable friendships which are *international* — and in the process, discover how to accept each other despite real differences, both by finding how much in common they all have, and by learning how to accommodate and respect the ways in which they differ. Conferences continue to be a force which keeps the Round Square flame burning bright.

No part of this history has been inevitable. At several times, Round Square has had to be sustained in the face of powerful opposing forces. Founded during Europe's years of postwar reconstruction, when funds were scarce in many countries, long-distance travel was less common and more expensive, and communications were far less advanced and accessible than they now are, Round Square immediately found itself struggling to sustain its message of global fellowship and respect for young people. The atmosphere of the Cold War era was not friendly to true internationalism, either.

Round Square also had to find a way to spread beyond its roots in the developed nations during an era in which much of the Third World was focused on throwing off the bonds of colonialism, which until recently had yoked many of these countries to the same nations where Round Square first took root. As an essentially student-centered, experiential, multilateral and hopeful movement, Round Square translated poorly into the thinking of educators in many nations at that time — particularly in countries where educational establishments were preoccupied with attempts to contain student unrest, make curricula uniform and prescriptive, enforce minimum expectations, and impose mass measures of performance. Round Square's individualized (and therefore heterogeneous and surprising) objectives of transformation and excellence seemed to fit such mass-education concerns poorly. And thus, while from a twenty-first century viewpoint and amid rapid globalization, Round Square may now seem to have been a logical, even prescient step toward educational reform, in fact for decades the entire organization looked odd and uninteresting to educators in many countries. And it did so for good reason — for much of what Round Square undertakes is still contrary to conventional thinking about schooling.

Of course there were also powerful barriers to collaboration that were rooted in national cultures (we might recall the final *caveats* in the two original "aims" documents). For instance, many citizens in the United States, until their 9 / 11 wake-up call, had felt little interest in making international understanding, global citizenship, or education for democratic responsibility serious priorities for secondary education.

Then too, other countries, such as South Africa and China, were for many years either preoccupied with internal political struggles, and / or had been frozen out of global relationships. And schools with a commitment to "internationalism" were not pleasing to all minds. One of the original Round Square schools, Anavryta, in Greece, was purposefully transformed by that country's new government following a nationalist coup, and as a result ceased to be a Round Square member. Even as I write these lines, obstacles persist. The post-Soviet social and economic disorders afflicting much of Eastern Europe have inhibited schools in that region from active participation. Ongoing turmoil in west Asia and many parts of Africa has had a similar effect. Yet, there is interest in all these regions. In time there will be Round Square schools there.

The challenges to be faced are not all located outside the organization. Round Square has repeatedly discovered barriers of it own making, and has had to overcome or bypass them in order to move ahead. Happily, some have already been addressed.

The most obvious of these challenges was a growing need to evolve Round Square's administration from something that could serve a small organization built on a shoestring, one which relied on implicit understanding within a group of closely-connected people, to something explicit, transparent, effectively managed, and universally understandable. This wasn't just a matter of scaling up to manage a larger enterprise. Round Square had to find a way to do business in a new manner, one which would be understandable to all groups, stable in the global environment, and could present a model of inclusive, democratic leadership and decision making.

The first long-term Plan for the organizational development of Round Square, formed in a consultative manner and approved during the Annual Conference at Starehe in Kenya in the early 1990's, was aimed at exactly these needs. It was a major step. The new design ensured that a growing number of projects and exchanges would be soundly arranged, safely led, and consistently evaluated, and that the central office would be able to manage the affairs of a larger community of schools and help them sustain relationships with each other. Moreover, Round Square was now empowered to build alliances with other organizations, raise and manage funds for the support of service projects and other activities, and communicate its message beyond the member schools' community. Subsequent Plans have continued to build on that foundation.

When he retired as Founder Director of Round Square in 1992, Jocelin Winthrop Young warned those who attended that year's Conference at Bishop's College School in Canada, about the need to deal with the remaining barriers to Round Square's development, as he then understood them. Some have since been overcome, or at least substantially attacked. For instance, he saw that the organization had outgrown its administration; but he knew a movement was afoot which would transform the staffing to be less "amateurish" and make processes more open and consensual. That, he correctly saw, would do much to make Round Square more inviting and accessible throughout the world. He also identified as a barrier to progress the failure to develop alliances between Round Square and like-minded organizations. Those he mentioned specifically in his address were "the other Hahn foundations" (Outward Bound, the United World Colleges, and the Duke of Edinburgh's Award Program), all of which were started or inspired by Kurt Hahn. Probably Winthrop Young could not have guessed that the other organizations were also aware of this need, or that a change was just around the corner. Discussions were soon underway, and a first joint conference of leaders of Round Square and the three other organizations named by Winthrop Young was organized by Terry Guest of Round Square in collaboration with Outward Bound Canada and Pearson College, and held in Victoria, British Columbia, in 2003. Cooperation among the groups now seems assured.

Other collaborative ties have since been developed, such as a substantial relationship with Global Connections, an international group of school leaders founded in the 1990's. Round Square's Executive Director has participated in the Global Task Force, an effort by the Board of Trustees of NAIS in the U.S.A. to design an appropriate way for that organization to lead American and Canadian independent schools toward less narrowly national views of education. Partnerships of this kind not only extend Round Square's influence, but also enrich its thinking. They should also, over time, aid Round Square by assisting allied organizations in doing their own work more effectively, thereby allowing Round Square to maintain its own focus and serve its own priorities.

In the same address, Winthrop Young accurately identified the theme of that year's Conference — "Celebrating Differences" — as a sign that Round Square was at last moving away from a tendency to see national, cultural, and linguistic differences as *obstacles* which needed to be "transcended" or entirely ignored, and was starting to accept them as *opportunities* — a rich resource of human diversity which, if addressed in a way which would enable students to identify, discuss, learn through and accept each other's differences, and more openly consider disagreements and conflicts, could be deeply educative. The development he identified has continued.

Two other barriers have proved to be less easy to deal with. Round Square has from the first used English as a working language. Doing so has benefited schools in Western Europe and parts of Asia, which have long taught English as a principal second language. It is also helpful to schools in countries such as India where, although other languages predominate in the home and street, English continues to be the language of instruction in schools for university-bound students. But Round Square's English-language commitment presents serious problems for schools located in countries where a mastery of English is less common among adults and less universally part of school instruction. It is not surprising, for instance, that the first Round Square member school in a Spanish-speaking nation, Markham College in Peru, is an English / Spanish bilingual school, and that Markham only became a full member in 2004. Round Square's English-first policy has had its most negative effect in *English*-speaking countries, especially the U.K. and U.S.A., where it tends to reinforce limited popular interest in foreign language study.

Certainly Round Square has made attempts to support multi-lingual education and to model linguistic diversity. One example would be the encouragement given host schools to use local-language terminology in Conferences. This has served to inject bits of vocabulary from several non-English languages into the glossary of the organization. But what is essentially token openness is by no means a solution. Can Round Square become more multilingual? (Should it *try* to be?) No one who knows Round Square would claim that this challenge is unimportant, yet none can say that it has been addressed in a conclusive way.

A second barrier yet to be crossed is the slowness with which the Round Square community's rich resources of perspective and intellectual diversity "penetrate into the classroom," to use a phrase of Winthrop Young's. What he was suggesting, it seems, was that classrooms were being walled off by teachers who might be "friendly [to Round Square] but uninterested" in taking the risks needed to make a collaboration between students, schools, and nations a part of instruction.

In all fairness, the difficulties teachers faced even at the time Winthrop Young was speaking were less of their own making and more complex than he may have realized. If anything, these difficulties have become greater since he spoke. The trend allowing domination of classroom teachers and instructional planning by government authorities, national examinations, and exam-driven curricula has by no means abated.

Nevertheless, the potential that Round Square schools have to link academic programs to the extraordinary international resource these schools possess is at hand, and enormously attractive. Were more done by Round Square in this one area, the result might have a powerful consequence — not just for instruction at member schools, but as a model which might have a positive impact far beyond Round Square.

Round Square's history suggests that another element will almost surely be needed for change to occur in relation to either linguistic versatility or academic collaboration. Until *students* are given the opportunity to help lead changes of this magnitude, the barriers which Winthrop Young saw as blocking the doors of Round Square's classrooms and limiting the support for language learning may well stay in place.

Chapter 3:
"IDEALS" at Work

During the early 1990's, it occurred to Judy Warrington, then the RS Rep at Bayview Glen School in Canada, that Round Square's priorities could be arranged into a most interesting acronym: IDEALS (International understanding, Democracy, Environmental stewardship, Adventure, Leadership, Service). Terry Guest, then Head of Bayview Glen, liked her idea, and began encouraging wider use of the "IDEALS" acronym. It soon began to appear in many of the organization's communications, and before long was a part of student conversations at Round Square schools around the world.

"IDEALS" provides a usefully brief explanation of Round Square's mission. It has also proved to be a fine way to ensure that *all six* priorities expressed in Round Square's statement of aims and objectives stay in everyone's mind as Conferences, projects, exchanges, etc. are planned, and as, year by year, Round Square is explained anew to students, parents, teachers, and the public.

Please keep in mind, as you read the following, that Round Square's "IDEALS" are *not* meant to be seen as a catalog of options which may be selected or ignored as one prefers! Rather, they describe a *single vision*.

I = International Understanding

> *It is hard to choose just one experience I have had as a result of Round Square! But I think that attending the Deerfield conference was special. It taught me that cultural differences and {different} backgrounds are **not** a barrier to international ties or the formation of great friendships. It also made me aware of how important having a common ground internationally really is...though I was already aware of some of this, it is now much a more important theme in my life.*
> — Female student, Australia

Each of the IDEALS can be seen as a "discovery learning" area which can be accessed through personal experience. Round Square schools guide students toward *international experiences* in at least three direct ways.

First, students at any Round Square school may apply for *term exchanges* with a member school in another country. A "term," which usually involves from eight to twelve weeks, has over time proved to be an ideal period for exchanges of teenagers, as long as mastering another world language is not the primary purpose. This period will be enough time for a student to feel he or she is "away" from home and from his familiar culture and friends. It also allows enough time to form relationships of some depth with peers in the school being visited. However, a "term" is not so much time that the dislocations caused by dissimilar academic programs are likely to become a major liability. It is also a short enough time to avoid the daunting visa problems which a number of countries now pose for students planning longer stays.

An exchange is experienced by a student in *positive* ways — it will be necessary to understand and adapt to a new country, new school, new culture, and new peers —and *negative* ways — a secure and familiar life is being left behind.

Both positive and negative challenges are frequently mentioned by students who have exchanged:

> *I went on an international exchange to England. It was important for me because I learnt to adapt to and appreciate a different culture than my own, while also being a proud representative of my own culture. I learnt that people can be very different…but it is in accepting their ways and cultures that true friendship can be developed.* — Female student, South Africa

> *My exchange to Australia showed me another way of life and taught me not only about others, but about myself. It showed me how to discipline myself without the aid of others doing everything for me.* — Female student, UK

> *I went on exchange for ten weeks to Australia. I expected it to be totally different from what it was. I am a Muslim, so I fasted in our fasting month, Ramadan. It strengthened my self-discipline immensely, and helped me to learn things about myself that I hadn't known. I also met people who came from many different cultures and learnt their ways of life. I will never forget my experience because it taught me a great sense of responsibility.*
> — Female student, South Africa

I went on exchange to South Africa and lived with a traditional South African family. It was the greatest experience of my life. They didn't all speak very much English so it was a difficult experience, but I learned so much about the language and the culture! I also made friendships that will last a lifetime.
— Female student, Canada

At times an exchange student's new environment and the one left behind merge in surprising and powerful ways. The following story was told me quite casually during a seemingly routine discussion on a sunny morning by a youngster who — until he began to speak — seemed almost the stereotype of Australian youth:

When on exchange in England, we took a school trip to Belgium to see Ypres on Remembrance Weekend. We visited Australian graves, but an English one stands out for me. This grave was in a small plot near a church, and belonged to an ex-student at the school where I was an exchange student. He was 17 when he died, one year older than I was, and had played at fly-back for the school's rugby team. I was filling the same position at the time...

I was struck by our similarities, and the remarkably different lives we led. I was asked to plant a cross on behalf of the school on the grave. This has become one of my strongest memories of my exchange. The experience left me more determined than ever not to support any form of conflict in the world.
— Male student, Australia

Where and how do we come to understand cultural differences? This student from Switzerland discovered the answer:

*During my exchange...I got acquainted with people of all different cultures and religions, particularly students from the Middle East. Their views and perspectives were entirely different than my own, and opened my eyes to people's attitudes, and how a person's behaviour and attitudes can reveal the differences in your culture and theirs. Just in the way we all tackled {the same} challenges, it became clear to me how different the people of the world are, and how we must really **work** to understand each*

> *other and live peacefully together.*
> — Female student, Switzerland

Exchanges also affect those who are visited:

> *A German student came and lived in our residence for a few months. It was a lot of fun and exposed the people in the house to a culture that was fascinating, and also completely different from our own. Round Square provides an opportunity for people across the world to connect, and to establish common bonds.*
> — Male student, Canada

Now and then students will add that going on an exchange requires a certain amount of courage — especially when one considers how absorbing activities and friends can be, and how anxious teenagers are when they leave an environment in which they are succeeding. These aspects of exchanging affect many youngsters, especially those who feel a strong responsibility to be successful:

> *{Last year} I exchanged to St. Philip's College in Alice Springs, Australia. It was very important to me to experience having the courage to be independent, getting to know other cultures, and also to represent my school in the most respectable and best way I could…which in my opinion I was able to achieve. I learned I could deal with new people, new situations, and new parts of the world. It was an amazing, life-changing experience!*
> — Female student, Germany

> *Going on exchange to Australia was an eye opener — I was the only black person in my town. I had to adapt to stares, etc…and {at the same time} we had to understand each other's differences — not only to live with {these differences}, but become empathetic towards each other.*
> — Female student, South Africa

In all cases the "home" school's screening process for a Round Square exchange is thorough. After all, the object is *educational*: a student will no more be sent on an exchange for which he or she is unready than they would be placed in calculus without demonstrating a reasonable mastery of algebra.

Assuming the "home" school believes a student will profit from an exchange, the RS Rep sends information about the student to possible host schools. RS Reps know each other well, have a common vetting process, and are accustomed to frank conversation. These conversations are critical because one of the primary jobs of RS Reps is to ensure that every exchange will end up placing "the right kid in the right school at the right time."

Exchanges, which involve no cost to the student's family other than for travel (increasing numbers of schools subsidize travel costs for students who receive financial aid), were once just what the name implies — a student for student swap. But now, what tends to happen is that the "exchanger" whom a school receives will not come from the same school that the student who has left will be attending. That's because the RS Reps maintain the exchange network as a sort of pool. The guidelines for this "exchange pool" are that the school / student match should in each case be appropriate, and the numbers in and out must balance for each school.

A second way international understanding is promoted is through annual Round Square Conferences, which normally last five to six days. A majority of participants must *always* be students. To date, all Conferences have been held at one or more schools, and all schools are expected to send a delegation to every Conference. Conference sites move around the globe in a deliberate fashion, which gives each Round Square school a "world campus." Recent locations have been:

Doon School, India
Bishop's College School, Canada
Rannoch School, Scotland
Schüle Birklehof, Germany
Southport School, Australia
Starehe Boys' Centre and School, Kenya
Westfield School, England
Athenian School, USA
Stiftung Louisenlund, Germany
Appleby College, Canada
St. Philip's College, Australia
Schüle Schloss Salem, Germany
St. Stithian's and St. Cyprian's Schools, South Africa
Deerfield Academy, USA
Ivanhoe Grammar School, Australia
Gordonstoun School, Scotland

Typically, a Conference will involve the following elements:

Major presentations: given by two or three important speakers on topics related to the conference theme. Themes are developed by a host school's student / adult organizing committee and proposed to the Executive Director for approval. They are expected to relate to Round Square's mission, as well as to a major world issue and the host school's locality. While the first truly dramatic use of a Conference theme was probably "Celebrating Differences," at Bishop's College School, Westfield School in England elevated theme to the level of controlling metaphor in 1997 with "Building Bridges," an idea which linked Newcastle's bridges over the River Tyne and its history of trade to Round Square's ongoing efforts to help students build their own "bridges" between people, nations, and cultures. That effort to use theme as a point of focus has continued. For example, the 2003 Conference theme, at St. Stithian's and St. Cyprian's Schools in South Africa, was *Ubuntu*, a word which can be translated as "I am what I am because of who we all are." Obviously, the struggle to create Ubuntu in a society which had until recently been cruelly divided between races met all the criteria for theme, and the theme's being stated in a language which was unfamiliar to most delegates was an especially effective idea. When former South African President and Round Square patron Nelson Mandela sent a televised message to Conference delegates that proposed this theme during the first moments of the Conference, a powerful experience had been staged.

Project presentations: students present reports to the entire Conference on RSIS and Regional service projects which have taken place in the prior year. These presentations, prepared in advance and rehearsed on-site under Ann West's guidance, usually include graphic overviews as well as summaries of what was encountered and accomplished. They are at once exciting as adventure stories, a resource of project and personal models, and a means for recruiting new participants for RSIS's ongoing projects. And they are also a way for a key Round Square program to be held accountable to its student constituency.

A *day of service and / or an adventure expedition*: delegates (adults as well as students) spend a day together doing service work (examples have included helping with a Habitat for Humanity construction project in South Africa, or at a soup kitchen in the USA), or engaging in a challenging outdoor adventure — a mountain climb, a canoe trip, a charity "run," or a back-country trek.

Large-group meetings with peer delegates (called *Riikas*, a Swahili word meaning "conference of equals"): Riikas are focused on practical matters having to do with Round Square programs and exploring ways to improve them.

Discussion meetings in small, mixed student / adult groups (called Barazas, another Swahili word, meaning "community meeting"). Several Baraza periods will occur during a Conference. Baraza groups, which are in all ways diverse, remain intact throughout a Conference. Each meeting will focus on a specific aspect of the Conference theme. Barazas are led by students from the host school.

Cultural presentations by students: These usually involve an art show, and music / dance / dramatic offerings.

Scheduled time for general mixing, socializing, and relationship building with peers from all schools and nations.

It has become usual for the "up front" roles at Conferences to be taken by students from the host school. Students are deeply involved in all aspects of Conference planning, organization and management. They greet arriving groups, share rooms, make announcements, lead discussions, keep track of who's where, and are the "voices" and the "faces" of every Conference.

Student feedback on Conference experiences suggests that this weeklong immersion in international fellowship can be deeply affecting:

> *During the 2002 Conference {at Salem} another student delegate — a girl my age — happened to bump into me, and {we came to know one another}. She led a life completely different from mine, but ... we bonded over our interests in music and art, languages and architecture...this, to me, is Round Square's most important function: giving students the opportunity to meet and learn from peers from around the world. My friend and I still keep in contact — just one example of the relationships Round Square succeeds so well in fostering* — Male graduate, USA

> *My experience at the {2003 South African} Conference broadened my view of people and the world. One particular activity stood out above the rest...one of our outings to Cape Town...to spend a day working with Habitat for Humanity, building houses in the Kilicher settlement {an impoverished "township" in which non-whites had been forced to live during the apartheid era}. Throughout the day we mixed cement, laid bricks, painted, and played with the kids in the neighborhood...it humbled me to see the reactions and interactions of foreign people who had not*

been exposed to an environment like this before. There was such a sense of community as we strived to take responsibility for humanity. There were many things which I learnt from this experience, but the theme of the Conference (Ubuntu) became very clear — a person is made a person through other people. I will always have this experience close to my heart.
— Male student, South Africa

*In 2001, I had a chance to travel halfway across the world to represent my school at the Conference in Alice Springs, Australia. It was not only the first time I left the country, but in a family of eight I was the first of my siblings to leave the country. At this Conference, my life was dramatically changed. I was however less impacted by the wonderful speeches...than by the stories of successes, failures, and achievements that all the student delegates had to share. I realized that no matter where one is and no matter how "bad" society may try to make us think some people are, deep down inside **we are all the same**. Deep down inside, we all have things that we love, things that we care for, things that we hope to accomplish in life — but most of all, each individual has a story to tell, each as unique and as fresh as even two pods from the same bean stalk are.*
— Male graduate, Kenya

I was nervous and apprehensive about what might happen at the Conference, and it turned out that many did voice their annoyance and disappointment with the United States. At the same time, they felt sorry — and hopeful — for us.

For me, this was really the first time that anti-American sentiment had been so apparent. It shocked me a bit, and tears flowed; but as I look back, I'm glad I was there. I'm glad they said what they said. I'm glad I was able to go to the Conference and hear first hand what people from elsewhere REALLY think. — Female student, USA

The 2004 Round Square Conference was pivotal in my understanding...I was completely unaware of the deep connections and friendships which could be established over such a short period. Just talking to people from different countries and sharing

stories about customs and cultural differences was an eye-opener. I now feel a little less ignorant about others, and am better able, from this first hand experience, to tolerate the beliefs of others who may not share my own point of view.
— Female student, Australia

We were in the middle of a two hour bus ride to the mountain that we were going to hike, and no one was talking. The boy in front of me was listening to headphones...so I tapped him on the shoulder. "What are you listening to?" I asked. "Punjabi music," he replied.. After further inquiry, I learned that Punjabi music is the Indian twist on American hip-hop and that this kid was the school DJ...

Considering that our conversation lasted the rest of the bus ride and soon engaged most of the bus, I learned the importance of little gestures. Asking one person one question conquered our big sense of awkwardness.

Finally, this experience was important because it represents my time at the Conference in a nutshell. Throughout the Conference, I found myself, time and time again, uncovering things I hadn't set out to uncover. That morning I left to hike a mountain, and when I came back not only had I summitted the mountain, but I had gotten a glimpse of teenage life in India.
— Male student, USA

The third direct way Round Square impels students toward international understanding is via international service projects. We'll deal with these under "S." (But the crossover between "I" and "S" is a first chance of many to point out how *all* these aims link together.)

A historical note may be helpful at this point. The founding of Round Square by an *international* group of schools, with the organization's prime movers based in nations which had recently been at war, clearly expressed the organization's "international understanding" objective long before any of its other "aims" had been written.

Certainly Round Square's "international" priority was, on a personal level, a consequence of the founders' own experiences during and immediately after the Second World War. Many had spent the last years of youth and the beginnings of early adulthood in military service. All had lost friends, loved ones, and peers. (Consider, for instance, Hahn's grieving statement at a postwar memorial service for Salem's war dead that, if all the graduates of Salem who had been killed in the war were alive and present, they would have filled *every seat* in that vast Abbey church). Beyond this, all involved had suffered through the immediate devastations of postwar life — not only physical privation and discomfort for the Europeans, but moral devastation as the true dimension of the Holocaust became known, the reality of the atomic bombing of Japan was better understood, and the world's swift slide into the Cold War began to make a third and even more catastrophic global conflict seem possible.

Sitting recently with Jocelin Winthrop Young, Round Square's Founder Director, in his retirement flat in Hohenfels, Germany, it was easy to see how a determination to build international fellowship for the young in the two countries where he had spent his life — Britain and Germany — had evolved on his part. On his wall was a photo of a Motor Torpedo Boat, and not far from it, a framed naval ensign. He had commanded that boat, which had flown the ensign, at the age of 22. In fact he had spent seven long years, starting after his graduation from Gordonstoun, as an officer in the Royal Navy, first in destroyers convoying supply ships from Sydney, Nova Scotia, to Britain during the Battle of the Atlantic, and after 1941 in Motor Torpedo Boats. Life expectancy in the Motor Torpedo Boats was even shorter than in convoy-escort destroyers; but at the war's end, Winthrop Young found himself alive, still in his twenties, and trained for only one career — the Navy — which he did not wish to pursue. He had seen more than enough of war to loathe it, and of wars between nations to feel powerfully about the importance of helping the next generation embrace alternatives to nationalism. Round Square was, for him and many others who created it, not just a way to bring about better schooling. It was a means for putting things right in the world.

That motive is still driving Round Square:

While attending the 1995 Conference in Australia I had the opportunity to meet students my age from parts of the world I knew nothing about, let alone had ever traveled to. The particular thing that happened to me was that the experience of living with and getting to know my peers from different parts of the world opened my eyes to what it is like to be from a different culture. I enjoyed discussion groups and socializing with other attendees — and made several long-term friends.

This experience of meeting people from "foreign" lands

in another country made me realize that there is nothing "foreign" about growing up in a different region of the world. It increased my understanding and acceptance of other cultures, which has made me a more open-minded and accepting person.
— Male graduate, USA

D = Democracy

*I went on a service project in India, and I learned my most valuable lesson from Diskit, a 17-year-old Ladakhi resident who taught me Ladakhi singing and dancing {while I taught her the American equivalents}. By the time we were beginning the Cotton-eye Joe and the Macarena, I realized that, after two hours and despite not knowing each other's languages and hardly being able to relate to each other's worlds, we were nothing more than two 17-year-old girls who loved learning to dance. What I learned from her and Ladakh was not how different, but how **alike** we are.* — Female student, USA

The most positive experience I gained with Round Square was about working together as a group {to raise funds for social service}. I had never imagined that just 15 people could be so creative, ambitious and strong! Above all, I had never thought that just a few teenagers would be able to raise 7000 Euros in a year…the way we organized events, and worked as a whole group constantly for a good cause of which we were all convinced, really made me aware that we can reach so much through teamwork and sharing! — Female student, Germany

Round Square's founders understood that a young person can't fully understand democracy and the democratic distribution of power without encountering and learning what power is in action — how it works (whether for good and ill), how one can appropriately and inappropriately use it, and how a group can collectively and fairly use power in a manner that will serve the good of all:

I was able to co-lead a Baraza group, something I had never done before. The students came from all over the world {and} the society in which each individual lives has different values…so a

short interaction would not change these values. But I realized that the purpose was not to change opinions, but to give {others} the opportunity to learn each other's views; not to argue ideals, but to listen, and, in time, adapt to the ideals of people sitting next to them. — Male student, USA

Perhaps the most important educational idea which the founders of Round Square took from Kurt Hahn was the *deliberate distribution of power to students as an educational strategy* designed to prepare them to use power capably and constructively in a democracy. The founders believed that the failure of western societies, including the major democracies, before and during two wars to protect humanity adequately pointed to a responsibility which schools — especially those which are likely to produce future leaders — *must* confront. It would be reasonable to say that what most startled and fascinated Jocelin Winthrop Young as he watched the 1954 service project in Greece was the way in which the students *effectively and generously used power:*

I have had many experiences with Round Square, from Conferences to an exchange in Australia. But one of the most memorable was planning for a Round Square Conference...the topic was "The Global Village: Celebrating Community through Diversity." It enabled me to work with students and teachers from all over the world, and really practice the true meaning of international understanding. In general, Round Square is what made my experience {at my school} so important.
— Female graduate, USA

Hahn proposed that the students at any school should collectively hold enough power so that failure on their part to use that power effectively and responsibly would seriously impair the functioning of the school. He also proposed that his schools combat entitlement. In his words, schools must "free the [children] of the wealthy and powerful from the enervating sense of privilege." "Those were the colors we nailed to the mast," one of the founding group has said to me. Such was the determination he and the others felt that students *must* be helped to see and understand the wise use of power.

The specific ways this strategy of educating for democracy through empowerment and "freeing...from privilege" works will vary greatly from school to school, for reasons that derive at least in part from differences of milieu. For example, we have looked at the Baraza meeting at Starehe, through which any student may respectfully raise suggestions or questions and expect them to be answered, and how this is tied to the school's carefully layered system for distributing power to and through student leaders. Athenian School also has a weekly school meeting, moderated by students and intended to give them power and voice. However, Athenian's dispersal of power and responsibility to students is usually accomplished through a wide array of committees rather than via a formal hierarchy. The contrasts are relevant to the different cultural contexts of the two schools.

At Deerfield Academy, a school we shall visit later in this book, Eric Widmer, the Head of School, believes that while Deerfield successfully meets many of the Round Square objectives, it is less than fully proficient in the "Democracy" part of the "IDEALS." At Round Square schools, when there seems to be underachievement, Round Square is almost always seen as *making a positive difference*, rather than marking a failure. Widmer remarked on the positive impact that the work of Deerfield students involved in the year-long planning of the 2004 Round Square Conference held at Deerfield had on the entire school. He saw a new wave of responsible awareness in the school which was still apparent months later. When I spoke with him, the school had just held a day of seminars relating to matters of race and ethnicity — its way of celebrating the U.S. national holiday honoring Martin Luther King Jr. "This was by far the most effective and ambitious of these Martin Luther King days," he said, "and we all were aware that this had a great deal to do with the experience of organizing and hosting the Conference." He particularly recognized the willingness of students (even those who knew their views might not be admired or understood by all) to speak frankly, listen attentively and respectfully, and try to understand why others thought differently.

A major challenge at many Round Square schools is to propose a life-style and set of values which will not just promote democratic views, but will effectively counteract the elitism and entitlement which can be outcomes of educational excellence. Because all Round Square schools have a commitment to providing need-based financial aid, many of the children who enter these schools do not come from privileged families. However, all who graduate are advantaged young men and women. While all of Round Square's "IDEALS" can be seen as ways to counteract entitlement, the way each school works to promote democratic values may be the most important.

Replacing entitlement with a respectful compassion for others is not an easy task. But students again and again report that such a view is unlikely to begin within the rather inexperienced and self-focused mind of the adolescent unless it has been triggered by concrete experience. Such an experience may be caused by something as ordinary as a dropped stone:

> *I was at Ladakh for an RSIS project, where we were building a community centre. Suddenly a rock fell on my hand, and it got bruised. I was in pain, so I went to the medical clinic for poor local people {which was a part of the same project}. But the condition of many of the people I saw there left me shocked — there were people with all sorts of terrible disabilities and illnesses.*
> *My pain vanished...*
> *This experience has had a long-lasting impact on me. I started to realize the pain and suffering which underprivileged people have to go through... while we who are privileged tend to care only about our own troubles.* — Male student, India

Democracy not only implies political empowerment of a population, but suggests fundamental challenges to each individual in relation to one's role in society and decision making. Round Square introduces students to these responsibilities in ways which can be transforming:

> *I was given the opportunity in my senior year to represent my school at the Round Square Conference in Canada. There I met students and adults from around the world. This experience made the world feel smaller and I felt more connected to the whole.*
> *The Conference provided me the opportunity to address an audience of about 500 people. I was so thrilled and proud to represent my school!*
> *I am still connected to that experience...I am now a teacher, and today I still talk about my experience.*
>   — Female graduate, Germany

E = Environmental Stewardship

> *After the project in India {we took a} five-day trek through the Himalayas. Northern India taught me to appreciate our own abundance of food and clean water. During the trek there was no vegetation, and any water came from {intermittent} glacial streams.* — Male student, Canada

What may be most interesting about the "E" of Round Square's "IDEALS" is that it was *not* part of the organization's mission in its early days. Environmental stewardship's emergence as one of Round Square's six primary goals happened because of student advocacy two decades after the movement began.

It has proved difficult to point to the exact moment when "environmental stewardship" was "officially" made the sixth priority in Round Square's mission. What is clear, though, is that, by the 1980's, "environmental projects" conducted by schools had become common and popular. An informational brochure published by Round Square in that period indicated that "environmental service" was a part of what the organization did.

Service projects aimed at least in part at conservation / environmental betterment had long existed, as undertakings by single schools, and (occasionally) by groups of schools. These included the construction and upkeep of public hiking trails, operation of recycling programs, and cleanup of the mess caused by oil spills. However, as the 1980's arrived, several schools began to mount sustained, multi-year "environmental" service projects which reached far beyond their own localities and were directly focused on environmental goals. The best known of these, Salem's "Boronka Project," has proved to be especially influential. This project brings students from Salem and, increasingly, from other Round Square schools, to spend a part of a summer holiday doing the heavy labor involved with restoring a vital wildlife refuge in Hungary which had been allowed to fall into disrepair during the post-World War II era. While this undertaking may seem identical to Round Square's other "service projects," in fact it was an important departure. The Boronka project was aimed at bettering the *environment for its own sake*, and teaching a deeper awareness to student participants of environmental issues, rather than doing these things as a means for providing relief to a needy group of people.

Perhaps because environmental stewardship had by then become a matter of concern and discussion for people around the world, and perhaps because of the location of the Conference, this issue was formally discussed at the suggestion of student delegates during the 1986 Conference at Salem, where the students reported on it as an important concern at the concluding plenary session. In the next brochure prepared by Round Square, in the early 1990's, the organization's environmental mission was explained more broadly and emphatically. At Round Square schools, it said, "projects, programs and curricula emphasize each student's destiny to be a caretaker of human society, and the planet's environment."

This revised commitment suggests that the Round Square community's thinking about "environmental stewardship" had progressed beyond environmentally-oriented service projects to a shared concern for teaching students the principles and issues involved with sustainability, and doing so in a way which would shape "programs and curricula" at schools, and the lifelong values of those who had attended these schools.

The ability of students to take the lead in revising the organization's core mission also is an example of what "empowerment" of students by Round Square actually *means*.

Currently, this newest of Round Square's goals may also be the least clearly developed programmatically. At the schools I visited in the process of preparing this book, when students and staff were asked to point to one area of "the IDEALS" where their own school and Round Square should be expected to do more, most named the "E" part of Round Square's mission. And while all could cite examples of environmental stewardship which were already taking place, many would also say that this remains the part of the "IDEALS" which most needs to be addressed in the years to come. In all fairness to these students and their schools, fascinating initiatives were already happening at each school. Moreover, there seemed to be no lack of enthusiasm or conviction on the part of adults or students about this objective. So it appears a safe bet that "E" will receive sustained focus and energetic development in the years to come:

> *I went to Hungary on an environmental project and experienced how **happy** you can be when you work to the benefit of nature...even when your help is little more than a drop on a hot stone.* — Female student, UK

> *The real benefit of the project was that we were doing something worthwhile to help the Hungarians establish their nature reserve. Our very presence lifted their spirits. We were the first truly international group to {work} at Boronka.*
>
> — Male graduate, UK

A = Adventure

> *At my Round Square school...we have an annual trip called "outweek" where we basically do outdoor education activities. One year the activity challenged my fear of heights by having us*

> *{be} dropped on a rope from a very high place. However, not only were we dropped from high up — it was my classmates whom I had to trust to hoist me up there in the first place and then catch me when I dropped.*
>
> *Afterward, I remember feeling just* ***great****! I had defeated one of my greatest fears and I had found a new trust in other people, and in myself.* — Female student, Canada

All Round Square schools ask students to participate in "adventure learning." What these adventure activities actually involve is amazingly various. Teams of students from Doon School climb beyond 20,000 feet in the Himalayas each year, just as the youngsters from Aiglon, in Switzerland, regularly go on Alpine mountaineering expeditions. Students at Sedbergh, in Canada, cross-country ski to rustic huts where they master the skills involved in winter camping. Students at South African Round Square schools share the "Saints Trek," a multi-day, rigorous backcountry / desert adventure. Lakefield youngsters all begin one of their school years with a week-long canoe trip on the wild rivers and lakes of the Canadian north. In the USA, Baylor students explore the undeveloped parts of the Tennessee River. Gordonstoun students climb in the Cairngorm mountains and sail the waters around Britain and the world in the school's ketch, *Island Spirit of Moray*. Appleby College in Canada has a northern "adventure campus" in the bush, for the same reason that Southport School in Australia has its outdoor education campus on unpopulated South Stradbrooke Island, at the southern tip of the Great Barrier Reef. A rite of passage for Athenian students is the Athenian Wilderness Experience, which involves a multi-day trek, including a "solo" day, in California's Death Valley, or in Yosemite National Park.

The list of school-based adventure programs within the Round Square community could go on and on. However, it is worth adding that adventure programs are not only school-based undertakings. All of the multi-school Round Square International Service projects conclude with an adventure-learning experience (called a "walkabout"):

> *{My school} gave me the opportunity to develop my passion for outdoor life into the business field, and my company…is the result of this. It also built my confidence, enabling me to face…whatever was thrown at me and gave me the ability to deal with people from all over the world.*
> — Male graduate, U.K.

What is so important about learning through adventure? A simple answer is that because *all* learning is to some extent experiential, and because adventure is inherently a high-intensity kind of experience, the potential adventure education holds to bring about *powerful* learning is substantial.

What kinds of learning may result?

My participation in the {Saints'} Trek was the most important experience I have ever had. It taught me about conquering emotion and {physical challenges} to reach a goal.
— Male student, South Africa

*During the Junior Round Square Conference we camped overnight, and it **rained**. This was important, because {the bad weather} made us all become closer to one another...I learned that sometimes all you need is {a situation like that one} to really meet other people — and to learn more about yourself!*
— Female student, Canada

While on exchange in Australia, I was invited to attend the school's annual "snow camp." This involved a week of cross country skiing as well as setting up camp in the snow, skiing with heavy backpacks, cooking for ourselves, and living without running water. Being a "little girl from South Africa" who had never seen snow before, let alone having been on skis, this was one daunting challenge!

By the end of the week we were expected to summit a mountain on our skis. After a week of telling everyone that I would never be able to do it, while tears of frustration fell with every second step, I managed to summit the mountain.

*The view from the summit was worth **fifty** weeks in the cold!*

This, for me, sums up Round Square: overcoming fears and frustrations, and feeling triumphant when looking back at the road one has just traveled...that's the "beautiful view" from the top of my own personal mountain!
— Female student, South Africa

More complicated explanations of the power of adventure / experience learning are possible, of course, and many have been advanced.

These range from Dewey's proposals (particularly in the late volume entitled *Experience and Nature*) to the developmental theories of Montessori, Piaget, and Vygotsky, to ongoing work on the relationship between human development, learning, and neuroscience. To some degree, the effects of these major currents of thinking about experience and education will be considered later in this book.

But for now, it may be sufficient to say that those who founded Round Square (some of whom were also involved with its sibling organization, Outward Bound, which shares a legacy of being an outgrowth of Kurt Hahn's work and thought), had ample reason to believe that these schools would be powerfully aided in their effect on their students if adventure learning were to have a role in their activities.

Since he was such a strong influence in this area of Round Square thinking, Hahn's view concerning adventure learning may provide a useful reference point. Hahn came to believe that team sports, while valuable (indeed, valuable enough so that he, like Deerfield's Boyden and Lakefield's Mackenzie, not only coached but *played on* student teams long after he became a headmaster), often disproportionately benefit students who have athletic talent. Furthermore, team sports do not always invite imagination, initiative, or personal commitment from each student. Thus, Hahn balanced the time given to team sports with time for "adventure learning" programs, such as hiking and mountaineering, or learning seamanship in fleets of "cutters" (large whaleboats, which could be rowed, or sailed with a simple ketch rig).

For Hahn, adventure education didn't imply that kids would just do what they wished. Far from it: adult experts taught the skills and disciplines which would be needed, vetted student plans, and oversaw preparations. Hiking groups, "cutter" crews, and other adventure programs would always have an adult or older student of proven skill and judgment nearby. Undertaken in such a way, adventure learning in his schools proved that the risks which attend adventure can be managed, and safety ensured, *without* diminishing the student's sense of challenge or adventure's learning potential.

Those who were present at the founding of Round Square knew that the real reason for supporting adventure education was not that youngsters need to learn how to climb mountains or travel by "cutter." Rather, it was that adventure programs offered an opportunity to "impel" students into selected challenges, where they would need to set objectives for themselves, struggle to meet their goals, assess their own successes and failures, and then move on toward new objectives with a clearer sense of their own developing capabilities and personal potential.

Adventure learning is therefore not to be understood in terms of curricular "content." Rather, it presents challenges which can enlarge the self-knowledge and sense of the possible of each young person who is involved. Adventure isn't a constant domain, either. It always begins just at the point where each person's fully mastered, understood world *ends*.

Students will sometimes describe adventure learning this way: *"it takes you out of your comfort zone."* What this tells us is that adventure education has the potential to tap into three of the most powerful urges felt by an adolescent — a hunger for self-discovery, a drive to explore one's limits and capabilities, and the need to take over responsibility for oneself. It should not be surprising that the result of learning experiences which capture the energy of these three universal drives can be so powerful.

Sometimes the adventure is a modest one:

> *I fell into a pool of mud on the expedition – but the experience was not important; it was what I learned from it! You can either be negative and make the situation worse, or be positive and turn it into a learning experience. That is what I did.*
> — Male student, South Africa

All of which invites this question: if adventure learning is so powerful and effective, why hasn't it become a universal practice at all schools? The two main obstacles to adventure education within schools are obvious: it competes with academic activities for students' time, and it introduces an otherwise avoidable perceived risk.

Adventure learning not only takes students away from more traditional, content-directed (and, in today's academic environment, "testable") curricular options. Sending kids to sea or up tall mountains proposes at least the *perception* of risk to their physical safety. Since both of these obstacles can translate into added costs, there is still another reason to say no: how is adventure education to be paid for?

It should surprise no one that only high-achieving, bold, confident, and adequately funded schools driven by a mission to "educate the whole person" are likely to take up the adventure-learning banner. And if these obstacles weren't enough, at least five other factors can block adventure education:

- Safe adventure learning demands that schools have an ample cadre of skilled adult leaders on hand, as well as competent administrative supervision of these leaders and their programs. Many schools feel they cannot meet this need.
- A school's faculty and administration must work together in such a way that they will consistently possess accurate knowledge about each student *as a person*, to determine what each student is and is not ready to take on. The culture at many schools inhibits such close focus on individual students.
- Few school Heads enter their jobs with sufficient training in adventure education to feel ready to take responsibility for it.
- Insurers have been known to oppose adventure programming.
- Governors must believe that each individual student's human potential justifies such an investment of time, money, and institutional reputation.

How risky is adventure education, really? Round Square (and its sibling organization Outward Bound) have long since proved that the actual risks can be minimized (nearly eliminated in most cases) via sound planning, good student / staff training, effective adult direction, appropriate investment in equipment and logistics, and strong over-all management. But even if adventure education's "perceived risk" is more a matter of perception than real risk, the time and money challenges which also attend adventure programming are real.

For all these reasons, no element of Round Square's approach to education is more deeply counter-cultural or apt to excite doubt and opposition than the "A" of "IDEALS," Adventure. Hahn's maxim (that students should be *"impelled* into experience") suggests very clearly what he believed the role of the adult educator should be (and, by omission, should not be) in relation to education through adventure. Round Square has never wavered from this purpose.

Hahn also promoted a saying which summarizes what, for the student, is always the most valuable product of adventure learning. He gave these words to Gordonstoun School as a motto: *"Plus est en vous"* — *"there is more in you (than you think)":*

> *At the end of fifth year we all went on a week's {outdoor adventure} course. Part of this involved rock climbing, which I had never done before...and did not believe myself capable of doing*

> *(what I said was that "it will ruin my nails!").*
>
> *But the staff coached me up every step of the way, despite my protestations and requests to give up. No way did they give up on me, and no way were they going to allow me to let myself off the hook.*
>
> *— And, you know what? I **did** it! I did climb that rock face (**once**)! They believed in me and that gave me the courage to do something I never thought possible.*
>
> *What I learned is that I am capable of **more**. I just need to push myself…oh, sweet success! To this day, I **know** I can drive myself more when I need to achieve that one bit more.*
>
> — Female graduate, UK

L = Leadership

> *While on exchange in England…we spent a day together working on leadership and team building skills. This involved problem-solving activities, a high ropes course, etc. Apart from thoroughly enjoying the experience and making new friends, I learned that it is just as important to have "followers" in a team as it is to have "leaders." When appropriate, I stepped back and let others lead — while at other times I was instructing the group.*
>
> *This has been an important understanding for me this year (my final one at my school) as I have at times been called upon to lead, and at others to follow. It takes patience to be a good "follower" — and humility to be a good "leader."*
>
> — Female student, Australia

The "L" part of IDEALS links to "leadership," although some Round Square schools use the term "guardians" to refer to major student leaders. In a democracy, a competent citizen must be prepared and sufficiently confident to be able to lead when leadership is needed by society.

"Guardian," however, is a word that not only has a literal meaning, but its own special place in the Round Square lexicon. The title given to top student leaders at several Round Square schools, among them Salem and Gordonstoun, is not "school captain" or "head boy / head girl" or "student body president," but "Guardian." The distinction made by this unusual title is not lost on students. A student leader has a primary duty to *protect and preserve* the community and those who live in it, not just to command. Thus, while the power to make things happen has been delegated to the student, so too has the responsibility to use this power in a way which is compassionate and caring.

Leadership is delegated in such a way that student leaders at Round Square schools will solve real problems and learn how to motivate peers. Here's just one example of how such delegation can work:

> *I was part of the Ladakh Round Square project. Our group was involved in building a community centre for the people of Chemdey. For this purpose, we needed to move a humongous ten-meter-long tree trunk {which was to be a main beam} over about two kilometers {without the aid of vehicles or animals}. At first it seemed impossible! But once we got thinking and co-operating with each other and acting as a team, everything began to work smoothly. We used more than a dozen support sticks to transport the tree: two people would hold each stick beneath the trunk, one on either side, and then the entire group would move forward, as if we were carrying a battering ram of some sort...{We succeeded and} it was amazing! This taught me that wonders **can** be achieved when we can inspire and organize team work.*
> — Male student, India

Opportunities to delegate leadership to students are always at hand; but knowing when they exist and daring to take advantage of them is by no means intuitive. The adult must be alert for opportunities and respectful of the learning they can provide. Even a baseball coach has opportunities of this kind:

> *An experience I had while on exchange was the chance to teach varsity baseball players at Deerfield Academy how to play cricket. The way they related cricket to baseball was rather innovative — and I found that I, too, learned a lot from this experience. I was able to see how things may look different from another set of eyes by observing the way they saw cricket as a game. This experience helped me to understand something: that what may be common to one may be most peculiar to another — and that a single thing {even a familiar one} can always be looked at from different angles.* — Male student, India

An ancient and, as research has long since proved, erroneous myth exists in many parts of the world that "leaders are born, not made." An even less respectable, but by no means vanished, myth suggests that males may be "natural" leaders, while females are not. Neither is so. Round Square schools do *not* subscribe to these disabling myths. All young people of both genders can learn to lead if given the opportunity, guidance, and respect needed to do so. All need to see examples of both genders being effective leaders. Round Square schools make these learning experiences happen.

Graduates of Round Square schools feel that the discoveries made through leadership during one's teenage years have a long-term value. One example comes from a graduate who is now an officer in the British Army, and a winner of the Military Cross:

> *Gordonstoun developed me as a whole person, and (as well as academic teaching) gave me the qualities I now require as a leader...{it} developed my knowledge, initiative, will-power, integrity and courage by setting me challenges in all sectors. The essential components included expedition, cruise, services and the sports field, as well as responsibilities in School and House. Without {this} grounding...I would be far less effective in {the} demanding role I now fill.* — Male graduate, U.K.

S = Service

> *I went on the Ubombo service project. Ubombo is a small, very underprivileged community in Kwazulu Natal. Our project involved helping to rebuild and improve the local primary school, as well as helping teach basic maths and other subjects at the high school...*
>
> *The experience as a whole was unbelievably {powerful}...it made me feel like I could improve and make a difference for a number of people even if it was in the smallest of ways. It also made me realize that I am coming from such a privileged background and that I didn't appreciate...things...like running water and having a meal to eat at the end of every day...*
>
> *The experience made me want to take complete advantage of the opportunities I have been given in life so that one day I can give help to more people who have nothing.*
> — Male graduate, South Africa

When the local children got out of daycare, they came running to see us at work. There was one little girl who became particularly attached to me. She had...sores all over her scalp, legs and feet. The road had pieces of glass strewn everywhere, and yet she was barefoot. I played with her, talked to her, taught her to say my name and "you" and "me."

I will never forget the look in that girl's eyes: hope, bliss, and wonder. She had nothing to complain about, and yet, if I were in her situation, I would have been endlessly complaining.

Since then, I try not to sweat the small stuff...and I have made it my personal goal to work with South African children as a resident pediatrician.
— Female graduate, Switzerland

If the "A" part of Round Square's "IDEALS" (Adventure) may be its least generally accepted and imitated objective in the context of the world's schools, the same cannot be said about "S – Service."

Service learning for young people has become a commonplace occurrence in societies on every continent, and while in some nations the institutional support for service learning is located *outside* the context of formal schooling, there are now few nations that lack respected service-learning programs of several kinds.

Service is also making headway as a legitimate part of schooling in many countries. In the United States, even amid that nation's ill-advised "back to the basics" movement, the highly influential National Society for the Study of Education devoted its entire 1997 "yearbook" volume to Service Learning.

It should not be surprising that of all Round Square programs and activities, service receives the most publicity, and is most frequently applauded. Service Learning is where Round Square began. Member schools have spent a half-century discovering how to make this kind of education work for students. The roster of the school-based major service endeavors for 2005 alone indicates the Round Square schools' "S" commitment:

- THAILAND – hill-village clean water project (Ballarat, January).
- CAMBODIA – "Sunrise" orphanage (Westminster, January).
- SOUTH AFRICA - nursery (Windermere St. Anne's & Wellington, February).

- THAILAND - working with a Hill Tribe (Regent's, February).
- COSTA RICA - environment/service/adventure (St. Clement's & Appleby, March).
- ST. VINCENT - community service project (Lakefield, March).
- BOTSWANA/SOUTH AFRICA - community service project (Lakefield, March).
- MEXICO - orphanage/environment/adventure (Collingwood, March).
- KENYA - work at Mekaela Academic centre, Mombasa (Louisenlund, March).
- PERU - stove building (Markham & Appleby, March).
- GHANA - community service (Athenian, March).
- VIETNAM - community service (Athenian, March).
- MEXICO - community service (Athenian, March).
- RUSSIA - work in orphanages (Salem, March/April).
- SOUTH AFRICA - Ubombo building/teaching project (St. Stithians, April).
- CYPRUS - environmental project (Hellenic, June).
- INDIA – Bio-gas plant/watershed development (Welham Boys, June).
- AUSTRALIA - environmental project (The Southport School, June).
- CAMBODIA - community service/house building (Ivanhoe, June/July).
- SAMOA – childrens' playground (Mowbray, June/July).
- HUNGARY - Boronka, environmental work (Salem, July).
- VANUATU - building project (St. Andrew's, July).
- BOTSWANA - environmental project (Cobham Hall, July).
- THAILAND – hill-village clean water project (Gordonstoun, July).
- ROMANIA - orphanages, community service (Gordonstoun, July).
- EGYPT - conservation work (Gordonstoun, July).
- SOUTH AFRICA - building project in Eastern Cape (St. Stithians, August).
- SOUTH AFRICA - service to disabled children/reading with farm children (Tiger Kloof, September).
- AUSTRALIA - Darwin, cultural project (Billanook, September).
- AUSTRALIA - Cairns, environmental project (Billanook, September).
- INDIA – Bio-gas plant/watershed development (Welham Boys, December).

To this long list must be added the larger RSIS projects organized by the Round Square central office staff, and always employing students and adult leaders from a wide array of Round Square schools: those in India (two projects each year), Kenya, South Africa, Scotland, and Thailand.

Service learning can be *transformational*. Again and again, not only students at Round Square schools, but graduates who are well beyond their years of schooling, report that service experiences have had a pivotal role in their own development, and in the formation of their values.

> *I had the opportunity to travel to Haiti in 1997 for a Round Square service project which opened my eyes to a different society, different people, and a different way of living. Having been somewhat sheltered from the "real world" this gave me a chance to see how lucky I had been and inspired a greater desire to give to others less fortunate than myself.*
>
> *At the same time, the Haiti project really helped me see that "giving" isn't simply about helping others to get where you are, but that this must be done within the context of each individual community you encounter. More recently I traveled to Zambia to work on a service program there — and I was prepared before I even arrived to recognize that {to serve effectively} you must work **within** cultures, traditions, and practices, and not attempt to impose your own.* — Female graduate, USA

> *At the beginning of the Ubombo project, as we were sitting under a big white tent, we were asked why we were there. It was a good question, which provoked thought — but also confusion for those who had no answers.*
>
> *I knew why **I** was there.*
>
> *As an underprivileged boy who grew up in the townships, poverty had become a friend of mine. But {my school} gave me a chance to become greater than what I could otherwise have been. And forever will I be grateful for that chance.*
>
> *Hence, when I thought ahead to the project, I saw it as an opportunity to give back, and to help those who weren't fortunate like I am.*
>
> *But helping and giving up my time really **wasn't** the main thing. For me, the project was more about learning {the truth} about other peoples' different circumstances...which were far worse than I ever thought they would be. It was those circumstances which made me realize how privileged and fortunate I am.*
>
> *Ubombo taught me in a week what others will spend a*

lifetime learning. — Male graduate, South Africa

While offering voluntary service at Kenya's biggest hospital I saw so much suffering…and also that you don't need to have money to give back to the community. Talking to the patients, encouraging them that there's a reason to have hope, making their beds, feeding them — all means so much. We **can** *make the environment and the world a better place, {if only} by caring for the sick and less fortunate among us.* — Male graduate, Kenya

Before being given the opportunity to go on a project, I felt reserved and unaware of the similar desire by each of us to do good, no matter our religion or ethnicity….{and} I was somewhat apprehensive. However, this soon diminished when we got down to the work of building new houses. I was touched by the kindness and genuine nature of the local people, and also by their respect for the job we were doing.

To think that we were a group of young people from all corners of the globe, helping to make life better for a small group of individuals, was amazing…it has taught me to look to the future and to the service of others, something I never really thought much of before coming to a Round Square school. I now understand the importance of service to others, regardless of whether I know them or not, and at whatever scale.

— Male student, Switzerland

At the beginning of this chapter, it was noted that programs driven by the Round Square "IDEALS" may touch on several of these objectives. The result of this linking of goals can be highly synergistic. In no area is such a fusion of the "IDEALS" objectives more likely to be present, or the resulting "synergy" more likely to occur in impressive ways, than in the international service projects which Round Square and its member schools conduct. It is not uncommon for these projects to bring an **I**nternational group together on a mutual and **D**emocratic basis; for **E**nvironmental goals to be among those pursued; an **A**dventure segment to be a part of the project design; and for all students to be challenged to **L**ead as well as to **S**erve. At least half of the 2005 projects listed above can be described as aiming at *all* six of the Round Square "IDEALS."

Why does this linkage of objectives matter? The best answer is one of teacherly pragmatism. *It works for kids.* It does because, for a young person, these goals are not really encountered as discrete and intellectually separate concepts, but in the ways they lead through experience to the emerging self:

> *During the project the group worked to improve the buildings of a primary school, create a craft centre for unemployed women, offer maths lessons to high school students, and in addition, delivered much needed food supplies and toys to the local hospital.*
>
> *It was this visit to…a third-world hospital that was my most important and memorable experience of the program. The experience of seeing not only poor and destitute people, but **sick** poor and destitute people, really moved me and helped me to realize, at the age of eighteen, the immense pain and suffering of so many people. This realization came at a time in my life when I was, like many teenagers, convinced that the world revolved around me. Having my world put into perspective and developing a deep empathy for others has powerfully impacted my life since then.* — Male graduate, South Africa

Sometimes an especially powerful learning outcome of an international service project is reported by a student who lives in the country where the project is taking place. Here's an example:

> *I went to do community service work with a group of people from many countries other than this one. That experience in one of the several thousand rural villages of South Africa was one of my first exposures to what life is **really** like for the majority of South Africans, and for most of the world's population.*
>
> *Aside from finding the work rewarding and enjoyable, I began to realize the responsibility the world's "privileged" have with regards to the "underprivileged." It is so easy to make a difference!* — *this experience taught me that. Since that time I've decided to study medicine and look forward to doing as much as I can for those in South Africa for whom medical attention is not now an option…I'm particularly interested in doing whatever it takes to change the AIDS situation that is ravaging this country.* — Male graduate, South Africa

More than a half century after a service project in Greece sparked the beginning of Round Square, voluntary service remains at the heart of Round Square's culture. At each Conference, reports from students who have taken part in the prior year's service projects are not just a part of the meeting's content, but energize new ideas for service undertakings, and revitalize the spirit of the entire community. At one presentation after another, students — empowered, compassionate, enthusiastic, and confident in the worth of what they are doing — seize the day, and they drive the organization forward:

> *In 2004 I went to a Karen hill village in northern Thailand, where we dug trenches for a kilometer through the jungle, laying water pipes as we went, and then built two 7,000-litre tanks in the village. We lived in huts with the villagers.*
>
> *The experience I gained will never be forgotten. The cultural experience, the team atmosphere, and the tough physical work all taught me patience, understanding, and real enjoyment. It was awesome!* — Male student, U.K.

Chapter 4:
Three More Schools —
Appleby College, St. Cyprian's School, The Doon School

IT IS A JANUARY EVENING IN CANADA. The snow underfoot makes the peculiarly loud, creaking sound which anyone from a wintry climate can interpret instantly. It is a sound which means *it's really cold.*

Yet on the Appleby College campus, bordering Lake Ontario, students walk about quite normally. Insulated parkas are only half-zipped. Many of the boys and girls are bare-headed, and below some girls' woolen skirts are unclad legs. The little groups hurry by, laughing and talking all at once, just as happy teenagers in every part of the world do. The only thing that seems unusual is that here, on this bitterly cold winter evening, clouds of steam trail the chatting kids.

These student groups are strikingly diverse. Appleby, in what is now suburban Toronto, mirrors the ethnic diversity of its part of Canada, where nearly one of every two adults was born in another country, and a large fraction of newcomers are non-European. Earlier in the day I'd been told that more than 40 nations of origin are represented in the families of Appleby's 630 students. But in their nonchalant embrace of winter, Appleby's students (even the large number of exchangers from other Round Square schools, some of whom are from regions where a snowy winter is beyond imagination) appear unified. Here, they seem to suggest, *we are at home. We may look and sound different, but we are one in dealing with Canadian winter.*

The near shore of Lake Ontario is a mass of broken ice, which now and then makes a groaning noise. What could be less urban, or more wild? Yet just a handful of miles to the east lies Canada's most powerful city, Toronto. The Appleby campus is large enough so that, standing at the school's center on this cold evening, one can almost imagine that this is still a rural school at the edge of the country town which Oakville was a century ago, rather than what Appleby now is, one of the nation's most prominent and selective schools, set in the midst of an affluent suburb near one of the world's great cities. At the same time, the school's complex relationships to the Canadas of myth and history, to today's mega-city Toronto, chic Oakville, and the highly competitive stratum of Canadian university-prep schools, aren't the only ways in which Appleby seems to be "on the edge" of a number of different social and geographic domains. In clear view across the lake are multiple pinpricks of light. Over there is the United States.

Appleby is also, quite literally, on another edge: it sits on a border separating two nations.

What's most striking about Appleby College, though, is the way in which, far from attempting to retreat within its sixty acres to escape the contrasting and conflicting aspects of its "on the edge" setting, it positively *embraces* its complicated place in history, the society of twenty-first century Canada, and a larger world. Creative adaptation to change isn't just a response to necessity at Appleby College; it could well serve as the school's motto.

"Canada's first e-school!" trumpets the Appleby website. "Academically vital! Globally inquisitive! Community spirited! Actively engaged!" Appleby College is a school which has entered the twenty-first century not just with confidence, but with *élan*.

That's not to say that Appleby ignores its roots. The school maintains a "northern campus" at Lake Temagami, well beyond the populous part of Ontario, which is used for adventure education in the Canadian wilderness (the Temagami campus has twice been the location of wintertime regional Conferences for North American Round Square schools' 7th to 9th graders). And when the school hosted the Round Square International Conference in 2000, students from all parts of the world were asked to bring rocks from each of their homelands to provide the makings of an *inukshuk* — a type of stone cairn traditionally built by the Inuit, natives of the Canadian north. Appleby's globally-sourced, jet-plane transported, student-built inukshuk now rises on a knoll at the south edge of its main campus, just above the lake.

Inukshuk markers, which often take an anthropomorphic shape, have long been used by native peoples as guideposts in the barren territories above the tree line in the Canadian north. *Here lies the path*, they say. The human-shaped inukshuk on the edge of the lake (and of Canada) symbolizes both the global organization's mission and Appleby's special character — uniting different peoples and cultures to accomplish something important. In so doing, the inukshuk (like Appleby) presents a guidepost telling other schools and other educational thinkers, "the path goes this way."

That kind of assertive confidence is characteristic of Appleby. Founded in 1911, the school had been in existence for eighty years when it joined Round Square as one of a wave of new member schools in North America. Yet when I asked students and staff about how Round Square membership affects their school, the responses suggested that Round Square is seamlessly fused with everything that Appleby is and always has been. They see Round Square less as a relationship for the school than as a part of its identity.

Students explained Round Square as a pervasive way of understanding and doing things. "You don't have to go half way around the world to be part of it," one said, thereby pointing out that Round Square is present each day as a part of ordinary school life. And although Appleby is very much what North American educators would consider a "multi-cultural" school, conversation with Appleby students may promote a suspicion that the "multi-cultural" term as used in the region reflects not just a disposition toward inclusivity, but also a rather shallow understanding of what a deep, powerful force culture actually is. For example: most of the Appleby students who had been sent on exchanges and overseas service projects tended to talk with me about the *cultural surprises* they encountered upon leaving Canada. One student who had been on a service project in Thailand commented on his surprise at finding that the destitute people he'd gone to help were in fact complex and courageous human beings, for whom he'd come to feel a deep, unanticipated respect. Several other youngsters talked about the impact a personal familiarity with the depth of human need in the third world had caused for them, and the equally powerful impact of the joy they had felt while providing shared service. "Happiness and need, need and happiness," added another. "That's what it's all about."

Teachers at Appleby see Round Square not as a separate and discrete program, but as a pervasive energizer of Appleby's mission. When I asked what the mission-based needs are that Round Square helps Appleby meet, their responses were immediate. For them, Round Square membership:

> Promotes empathy
> Encourages global awareness
> Helps to build world citizens
> Supports the school commitment to service
> Integrates well with social-science curriculum
> Builds real international friendships
> Helps to develop critical thinking
> Benefits individual growth via adventure and responsible
>   risk-taking

All these products of Round Square affiliation relate to Appleby's core mission. "Round Square isn't just a network," one teacher added. "It's a network that *works*." "It expands our vision," said another. "And the whole community believes it's important — leadership, faculty, support staff, kids, families." When I asked them what they'd like to see as targets for Round Square at Appleby in 2015, they agreed on three priorities: Round Square will actively involve *all* students and faculty members; it will involve graduates in significant ways; and parents will not just be "in the know," but ways will be found to help them become *productively* engaged.

The RS Rep at Appleby, Rob McGuiness, agreed with his fellow staffers' and students' perceptions that Round Square is "really integrated" in the school. McGuiness is encouraged by school leaders and his colleagues to "think of every kid as a Round Square student" even though individual students may be involved with Round Square in different ways at different times during their years at Appleby. Although he finds little resistance to the program for which he advocates, that doesn't imply there aren't problems to be addressed. The one that most concerned him when we spoke was the apparent "unreadiness of some students to adjust reasonably well" when they arrive on service projects. The initial adjustment for many youngsters appears to be hard. The result in a few cases has been a less productive experience than he'd hoped to see. "We need to think about how to prepare them better," he commented. This willingness to engage in "positive self-criticism" is a characteristic I observed in others during my time at Appleby.

As a person who is continually asked to explain Round Square, McGuiness was especially pleased to hear about this book. There is a need, he said, to help both educators and parents understand "the importance for youth in today's society of having their eyes opened to experiences which will help them develop values and attitudes they will need if they are to make a positive difference in the world." Just as important, he said, is helping parents understand the "importance of challenge as a key part of growing up — that a child's having a bit of discomfort may at times be a *good* thing."

The wholesale enthusiasm about experiential learning and international ties which I heard from all sectors of the student body and staff at Appleby College very much extended to its Head of School, Guy McLean. McLean fully shares his colleagues' long-range aspirations regarding his school and Round Square, and their concern that its current impact must become more inclusive and powerful.

When we spoke, McLean was developing plans to make participation in a major service project a formal graduation requirement. One hurdle will be how to fund this universal expectation. Currently, at Appleby as at most Round Square schools, the added cost of a service project for children of families who pay full fees must be assumed by the student's family (students who receive financial aid can expect to receive an appropriate level of assistance). However, while parents of all children taking part in service projects must give their approval in order for a child to participate, the separate cost-assessment process has tended to frame service in the eyes of some fee-paying parents as an activity which is less than a central expectation of the school, more an "option" residing outside the main curriculum. For some of these parents, particularly those who fear that a one-time added assessment will be beyond their means, this billing structure invites opposition — which can even, now and then, lead to an outright refusal to approve international service.

What McLean hopes to do is to pair announcement of a formal international service requirement for all students with a step to include a pro-rated portion of the cost of a student's participation in each year's basic school fee. Doing so should help parents financially, by spreading the cost of international service projects across all years the child will be at Appleby. Moreover, it should help clarify for prospective parents that participation in service is an *intrinsic part of education at Appleby*, not an "add-on." Heads of other Round Square schools will be watching closely to see how this proposal fares.

During my time at Appleby, I spent part of an evening in discussion with an alumnus of the school who spent a final year of secondary schooling at Appleby following his graduation from Starehe, in Kenya, and prior to his attending a university in Canada. The following excerpts from my notes of that conversation epitomize what the impact of a Round Square education can be for one young person:

> *You know, in 1996 I was in a dilemma. Thanks to Starehe, I'd been given access to a level playing field in terms of my future in my country (not in dollars, but otherwise). Having been at Starehe made me able to see all this — to evaluate what I could do, and what I might do for people.*
>
> *Round Square put that thinking in a larger perspective. I began to re-examine how I should "reach high" {referring to "natulenge juu," Starehe's motto}.*
>
> *After I was invited to come to Appleby, I began to realize that what I had to confront was a fear of the unknown. That was the dilemma I had to reach past to "reach high."*
>
> *Of course time has passed since then. I am now an executive with a leading high-tech company {he had just been told his next assignment would be oversight of the company's*

operations in East Africa}. Do I like what all this has done to me?

*How do I say "no" in a positive way? As a strong yes? It's challenged a lot in me — how I live, eat, look at people, and judge them; but it's brought me much closer to **me**, as a spirit.*

I meditate about this a lot, especially about this realization — that to live, I must be challenged; but I must also see the people about me smile. **Both.**

In effect, that's where Starehe and Round Square have taken me. They have given me the ability to think, and live, outside the box.

§

In 1996, when I first visited St. Cyprian's School, a 135-year old Anglican girls' school situated at the foot of Table Mountain in Cape Town, South Africa, I was mid-way through a sabbatical term away from my regular job. I was there to observe how independent schools in South Africa were dealing with life immediately after apartheid.

It was, to say the least, a tense period. The old government had just been replaced, and the Truth and Reconciliation Commission's work was underway. During my time in the country the Commission had reached a standoff with a leader of the old regime. No one knew what would come of this impasse. Meanwhile, the danger of ethnic and sectarian conflict was on everyone's minds, whether the subject of worry on a particular day happened to be bitter Afrikaners, angry Zulu nationalists, or dissatisfied Muslims. Some members of the latter community, many of whom are located in the Cape Town area, were at that moment engaged in strident, sometimes violent protests. The news each day was full of reports of gang-based crimes, ranging from robberies to murders and rapes. Even modest homes were surrounded by razor-wire crested walls, on which were posted signs threatening "armed response" to trespassers. In more affluent areas, the providers of "armed response" often were visible.

Not surprisingly, at school after school which I visited at that time, I had to pass through heavy gates manned by gun-toting policemen in order to enter the grounds. Security personnel could sometimes be seen patrolling.

All in all, 1996 was not a time when most South African schools presented themselves to visitors in a way which reflected confident engagement with a larger world, or even with their own neighborhoods.

Yet when I had arrived at St. Cyprian's, the front gates were open. There were no armed guards. Yes, it was the end of exam week, when most teachers but few students were present; and yes, there were two groundsmen working just inside the gate, who immediately (but with smiles) came up to my car and asked me whom I was looking for...one then put down his rake and guided me to the school office. But still, the contrast was startling, especially as St. Cyprian's is not set in an upscale suburb or in the country, as were many schools I visited. It is an urban school, in the Oranjezicht neighborhood of Cape Town.

Something about this school was *different*.

While waiting to see the Headmistress, I looked through school literature. What caught my eye was the school motto: *"we teach not for school but for life, we train not for time, but for eternity."*

Life and eternity! We are *not* talking about a vision which ends with exam results or university placement. Even at such a difficult moment for schools in South Africa, St. Cyprian's was looking far beyond the immediate moment. What this school was doing suggested a bold, confident focus on the future which, I came to realize, is a distinguishing characteristic of St. Cyprian's.

When I met with Tessa Fairbairn, the Headmistress, in her office in the old Dutch-colonial-style building that is the center of the school, she reflected the same long-range view, and a profound confidence in her school and her country. Yes, she said, of course there were dangers with an open gate; but the staff were watchful; so too were the neighbors. Yes, things were dicey in South Africa; but they would not always be so. And yes, challenges lay ahead for independent schools; but they could and would be overcome.

At that time, St. Cyprian's was not yet a Round Square member (due to Round Square's policy of admitting no South African school to membership until a change in governments had occurred). Yet Ms. Fairbairn was utterly sure that St. Cyprian's would be a member. She told me she had carefully studied Round Square, and that in every way except formal membership, St. Cyprian's was "already a part" of the group. Wasn't it time for this implicit Round Square "membership" to be properly recognized?

Bold as her claim may have been, my subsequent observation found no indication that she was overstating her case. Quite to the contrary. Although the political isolation of South Africa had frustrated the school's enthusiasm about internationalism, in every other way the principles underlying Round Square's "IDEALS" were visibly present at St. Cyprian's. This had long been so. And at a time when some independent schools in South

Africa were being driven by panicked parents to become whites-only sanctuaries, St. Cyprian's was deliberately following its own abiding mission, which was taking it in precisely the opposite direction.

Here's how Archbishop Desmond Tutu describes the character of the institution:

> *St. Cyprian's is a school which has consciously striven for excellence without elitism and has achieved this delicate balance.*

Fast forward eight years to November, 2004. I am once again at St. Cyprian's, but this time to interview students, graduates, and staff for this book. None of the post-apartheid challenges has vanished. However, progress in the nation is visible in many ways, and certainly the sense of overwhelming crisis has eased. St. Cyprian's is thriving. Beyond that, its way of explaining itself in relationship to the South African context is no less bold or confident. Here, for instance, is the school's explanation of its aim to educate young women who will "make the difference:"

> *The unifying vision of the African idiom Ubuntu Ngumuntu Ngabantu – "I am because you are: a person is a person through other people" is the essence of "making the difference." We co-exist with others, we live in community; we listen, we hear, we care.*
>
> *We believe that children need to understand where they fit into the greater scheme of things and that it is necessary to engage with the world out there, because we can, each and every one of us, contribute to the well-being of the community around us. St. Cyprian's girls are proactive in making the difference.*

Now formally a Round Square member, St. Cyprian's is one of a growing group of schools in Africa which are "making the difference." Its students have been plunging into international exchanges and service projects, and are quick to say how much they have been learning:

> *{A current student, referring to a recent exchange to a school in India}: I learned so much — especially about cultures, and how completely different cultures can be. I thought I understood a lot about this. What I quickly learned is that I didn't know **anything**.*

At the same time, students reported about how exchanging to other schools had clarified their perception of St. Cyprian's. The following was said by a student who had exchanged for language study to a (non-Round Square) school in France. Her view says at least as much about the values and daily priorities she had come to see as "normal" at St. Cyprian's as it does about the school she attended overseas:

I was appalled at how academics and competition pushed all else out of that school's life. It was really sad.

When I asked a group of St. Cyprian's girls to suggest a phrase describing Round Square as they knew it through their school, these were some of the responses:

Challenging convention
There's more in you than you know
For life
Self-discovery
Global village
Discovering your heart

While St. Cyprian's girls do many of the same types of service and adventure activities that all other Round Square students undertake — they rebuild homes with Habitat for Humanity, tutor needy children, volunteer in civic service organizations, white-water kayak and trek in the northwestern desert, just for starters — they have also developed innovations of their own. Several years ago, St. Cyprian's students began an effort to sell beadwork badges made by AIDS-infected mothers of small children as a way of raising money to help these sufferers live decently and care for their families. With the eventual partnership of students at many other Round Square schools around the world, vast numbers of these badges have been sold, and substantial amounts of funds (at the time of this writing, many tens of thousands of US dollars) had been collected. More recently, students began what they call the "Girl Child in Afrika Campaign," aimed at dramatically increasing the amount of financial aid St. Cyprian's can provide to needy girls. This program involves distribution and sale of village-crafted "Girl Child dolls" on every continent. Again, the results have been impressive, and demonstrate that students at a school for only 750 young women between the ages of 3 and 18 can, even if the school is in a developing nation in Africa, truly "make the difference" in substantial ways — *if* the latent capabilities of the students are respected, their ambitions and achievements celebrated, and every student "buys into" the strategic goals of the institution which they attend.

You may recall the seven "Laws of Salem" which Kurt Hahn posted for his teachers to study. At each school I visited I asked students and graduates to assess the relative importance of the Hahn "laws" in the context of their own life experiences, their own school, and life in the twenty-first century. The fifth of these "Laws," *Train the Imagination*, often puzzled students. How, they wondered, can someone "train" an intangible entity like an *imagination*?

But the St. Cyprian's graduates with whom I spoke understood what this phrase meant. They had *seen* how imaginations can be "trained." They found this precept not only understandable, but one of the most important of the "laws." As they explained their views, it became clear that St. Cyprian's "trains imaginations" through active experience, by encouraging the kind of student leadership, compassionate entrepreneurialism, group work, and purposeful risk-taking which has enabled teenaged girls to take on ambitious and successful philanthropic efforts like the AIDS badges and Girl Child in Afrika campaigns.

At St. Cyprian's, as was the case at Appleby, the Round Square Rep's view of Round Square's place in the school amounts to seamless integration (at St. Cyprian's, the "RS Rep" is actually a team of three). They described Round Square at St. Cyprian's as "welded in...broadly based...not an add-on...connected." Students have a multitude of opportunities for involvement and challenge, within and beyond the school. They mentioned support from the school's Board of Governors, as well as from the Headmistress, and growing interest among colleagues at other schools in Cape Town. All felt that the time was ripe for one or more RSIS international service projects to be based in South Africa (this step has since been taken).

A conversation with Ms. Fairbairn and her Board Chair, Anthony Haggie, was an interesting follow-on to the talk we'd had eight years earlier. While in no way diminishing the strength of the "claim" she'd made for Round Square membership at the earlier date, Ms. Fairbairn now saw that active membership had brought surprising benefits to her school. It had "greatly accelerated and consolidated" the school's progress toward the goals she and her Board had been pursuing. Her Board Chair agreed. Round Square membership had, according to both of them, enabled St. Cyprian's to become more powerfully *itself*.

A few months before I visited, the school had held its annual Africa Day chapel service, during which a moving speech by President Thabo Mbeki was read. It concluded "today it feels good to be an African." Creating a sense of shared identity among all the different elements of this diverse institution is one of the school's goals. This is how that goal shapes St. Cyprian's involvement in an international community of schools:

> *It is only by knowing who we are and where we come from that our learners are able to significantly, effectively and with humility reach out to the international world. Thus, firmly grounded in the spirit and generosity of this land, we make connections, share experiences and thoughts, forge new relationships and cement old friendships with those from other lands.*

It is impossible not to feel hopeful — indeed, *confident* — about South Africa's future after spending a day or two at St. Cyprian's School.

§

When, in 1980, the leaders of Round Square were trying to invent a way to replicate something like the disaster relief project in Greece which had sparked the movement's beginnings, they realized that they would have to find two key elements: a "base" school which could provide local knowledge and logistical support, and a more or less ongoing disaster (or long-term need for service) as an objective.

Anavryta, the school which had been the "base" for the 1954 service project, had been lost to Round Square as a result of a coup in Greece; and while many of the other member schools would have been happy to be "bases," and some had done so effectively on occasions (for instance, during the period following the Amoco Cadiz oil spill), disasters in western Europe and North America were infrequent and unpredictable, and in those regions, Round Square schools were still few in number and widely scattered.

It was suggested that a variety of projects might be located in India; and that, if this were to happen, The Doon School, a famous boys' boarding school in northern India, which had earned a reputation for service by its students, might be an abiding "base." Doon was not then a Round Square member, and had not even indicated an interest in membership; but nevertheless, contacts were made with Shomie Das, the future Headmaster of Doon, and his predecessor, Gulab Ramchandani.

They were asked two questions. Despite the fact that Doon was not a Round Square member, would the school be willing to serve as Round Square's logistical "base" for a series of international service projects in India? Secondly, would Doon lend these projects a few skilled members of its staff and some capable students to provide local knowledge and leadership? Doon's answer to both questions was immediate: *yes*. Taking part in such an undertaking would fit the school's existing mission well. Round Square's next question was phrased in a more circumspect, careful way. Could Round Square really *count on* there being appropriate needs to bring students from other parts of the world to provide service in India, year after year, given that plans and travel commitments would necessarily have to be made long in advance?

Shomie Das's reply was made with characteristic humor: "In India, my friends, no matter what the time of year may be, there not only are needs to be met, but we will *always* have a disaster to deal with. You needn't worry about that!"

And so, with Doon's help, India became the place where Round Square's long-frustrated determination to develop an ongoing program of international service experiences for students finally became a reality. And this step also began a process which swiftly led Doon (and a number of other Indian schools) to join Round Square.

Founded in 1935, by Indians, at a time when India was still ruled by the British, Doon was meant from its inception to be a school with a purpose — and that purpose was, and still is, deliberately connected with India's destiny as a nation. Doon was designed to develop the highly skilled, generous, compassionate, and courageous leaders from all strata of Indian society whom the country would need in its future as a free-standing nation. Doon's founders were determined to develop a school which would be academically second to none; but while it might borrow processes from traditional boarding schools, it would do so in ways which were distinctively Indian, and directly related to its mission to be a crucible for leaders of the nation. In keeping with that goal, Doon has from the outset been national in its student population, and ethnically and socio-economically inclusive, rather than being sectarian, regional, or class / caste-based. And since, in a huge nation, Doon's relatively small annual cadre of graduates can never hope to make a difference through force of numbers, it was obvious that they would have to do so through skill, ability, energy, and strength of character. Thus, the cultivation of those personal qualities in every Doon student became a major goal.

Out of these objectives grew Doon's distinctive ethos and unusual co-curriculum, one which was aimed at objectives which closely resemble those summed up by Round Square's "IDEALS" acronym. Among them is a commitment to voluntary service for all students. The Doon term for this requirement is "SUPW" — "Socially Useful Productive Work." This was the aspect of the school which led Round Square to ask for Doon's help in the first place.

One might even think of Doon's deeply purposeful approach to service in relation to Archbishop Tutu's description of St. Cyprian's as *"a school which has consciously striven for excellence without elitism and has achieved this delicate balance."* In India where, even now, many children remain uneducated or undereducated, youngsters who are lucky enough to be as well educated as a graduate of Doon automatically become an elite. Doon's determination to seek its own "delicate balance" by providing educational excellence within a context designed to promote *non-elitist* values was farsighted in 1935 — and in India and most other nations of the world, it still is.

The school, which has just under 500 students, is located in Dehra Dun, an old garrison town which is now the bustling capitol of the far-northern province of Uttaranchal. This city is the main urban center of the Doon valley, which marks the geographic transition between India's northern plains and the Himalayas. The front range of the Himalayas stretches along the horizon of Dehra Dun. These great mountains are alluring — and have always summoned the adventurous spirits of Doon boys. Hiking and mountain climbing are major activities at the school. Student-led weekend trips into the hills and mountains occur frequently, and each year the school sends expeditions of students on climbs above 20,000 feet in the high peaks of the Himalyas. It has been said that Doon and its graduates have been the most significant force in the development of Indian mountaineering. Perhaps that specific bit of the school's reputation wasn't in the minds of Doon's founders, but the bravery, skill, daring and prudent leadership which must be involved in any successful mountaineering expedition certainly were! Much of the part of India which remains forested lies near Doon. That the school's lovely campus was formerly the home of India's forestry college is evident in the great specimen trees which rise above its beautiful grounds.

Why, I asked a trio of Doon's staff members, had Doon become involved in Round Square? What is the product for the school? These are some of the answers I noted:

Internationalism: Round Square invites, assists, rewards and promotes it;

Partnership for students with young people from all the other schools "breaks myths" — both about First World infallibility, and about third world inadequacy;

Round Square helps Doon students feel capable of acting globally, with confidence;

The international projects (both in India and abroad) build a greater awareness of universal humanity;

Projects are a great morale booster; the boys are excited about them before, during, and after;

Exchanges (both to and from Doon) have over the years become a huge benefit to the school.

What then, I asked, are the major difficulties / challenges for Doon and Round Square? They concurred on four:

Sustaining the worldwide intensity of conviction, and the sense of "brotherhood," as Round Square evolves, grows, and its leaders change;

Raising awareness that "the choice of the Round Square Rep at each school is much more crucial than the choice of any other leader or member of staff;"

Managing both the existing and future size of the organization effectively;

Finding funds to maximize participation for students (a problem in all countries, but a huge problem in third world schools).

I posed the same questions to Dr. Bajpai, Headmaster of Doon. While he did not disagree with the staff members' perspective, his more strategic view is an interesting extension of their views:

The annual Conference has proved to be "a great ingathering" — not just a reliable booster of enthusiasm, but it creates a most healthy kind of "intellectual churning" for students.

Exchanges are increasingly valuable. The school was, in the past, "rather insular" in its deliberate focus on India. Round Square has proved to be "a guide opening out" and "a great reassurance" because of its affirmation of the enduring Doon values.

The effect on Doon's own service tradition has been extremely valuable. Involvement with Round Square has "multiplied and invigorated" Doon service projects, and has helped both students and staff better "mediate cultural differences" via service.

Asked about difficulties and challenges, Dr. Bajpai indicated these key issues:

> Promoting exchanges to Doon — these have increased, but more would be welcome;
> Finding ways to make Round Square "even more intellectually enriching "— by challenging students regarding multiculturalism, taking risks around politically charged issues, and "shaking the universe" of student thinking;
> Addressing limitations regarding numbers of students who can go on exchanges; and
> Finding resources to fund Round Square experiences for a larger number of needy students.

During my visit to Doon, I was able to have a sustained conversation with a group of fifteen Doon students concerning similar topics. Like virtually all students at Round Square schools around the world, they felt that the most important aspect of Round Square is that it leads to "self-discovery." However, they were a bit unusual among the student groups whom I interviewed in that they also believed that experiences relating to the "IDEALS" are highly effective in "training the imaginations" of students. This, I suspect, had as much to do with the contrast of Round Square's experiential curriculum to the highly-focused academic regimen that is usual in top-level schools in India as it was an assessment of Round Square, per se.

I asked the students to make a one-phrase definition of Round Square. Here are some of their suggestions, in the order they were proposed:

> *An experience!*
> *Bridging of worlds*
> *An organization for tomorrow*
> *A common cause*
> *Helping hands*

Only at the end of the list did someone add *"About you and me."* Clearly, what first springs to mind with this group when defining Round Square is what the student *does*...not the educational motives which may lie behind that activity.

On another occasion, I walked the campus with a pair of older Doon students, listening to their comments as we ambled past inter-house cricket matches (a serious affair: one Doon graduate, a former international cricketer, told me that these contests are not only well played, but are *far* more important to students than any interscholastic match could ever be). It was a lovely spring afternoon, sunny and warm, and the school grounds seemed a green, tree-shaded paradise below a skyline of mountains, even if high-rise apartment buildings could be glimpsed in the distance and India's amazingly variegated, chaotic but (mostly) non-lethal traffic chugged, wheezed and honked beyond the gates. We poked into labs and classrooms, state-of-the-art computer facilities (a much-promoted Doon strength — virtually all of Round Square's publications are edited and assembled for publication by Doon's students and staff), and an outdoor theatre built years ago by the school's students. Outside the impressive arts center, music students relaxed during a rehearsal break.

Both of my student companions had been on exchange to Round Square schools in First World countries during the prior year, and they spoke about these experiences with a mixture of great politeness and look-you-in-the-eye candor that is very much a trait of Doon boys. While they were both bright, competent, and capable teenagers, it soon became clear that exchange had been a stirring challenge for both of them. Each was confident that he'd done well and "learned a lot," but neither had stopped assessing what had been experienced and accomplished, what to think of the places where he had been, and what these assessments said about India, Doon, and himself. While what one RS Rep has called "the long debrief" is a universal phenomenon for Round Square students who've returned from exchanges, this wasn't the first time I had sensed in talking with students from a less-developed country who had spent a term abroad that exchanging from the under-resourced but also more settled and stable culture of a third world country to the more affluent but also less stable and more amorphous culture of the First World can be a *very* big leap. To paraphrase Doon's Headmaster, it had been a "universe shaking" experience.

One of the most striking aspects of Doon as an institution isn't visible on campus at all. It's the extraordinary network of graduates who by now lead many of the country's social, cultural, service, and technical organizations, and its government (one alumnus, Rajiv Gandhi, was a Prime Minister, and it's a good bet he won't be the last Doon graduate to hold that responsibility).

Rather like its Round Square siblings, Kenya's Starehe and Peru's Markham College, Doon is a school with an avowed nation-building mission. As a seventy-year-old school, it is merely a bit farther down that road. The graduates of these schools know that a mission "to make the difference" is part of the burden which comes with a diploma from the school, and they seem to accept it. However, through Round Square, Doon like Starehe and Markham is recasting the idea of building leadership for a nation into one of developing leaders for the world.

Before leaving Dehra Dun, I was able to talk at length with Gulab Ramchandani, former Headmaster and graduate of Doon, who — now in his 70s — is his country's most respected educational adviser and consultant. I asked him a few questions how Round Square functions in India:

What has drawn Doon, and other Indian schools, to be involved with Round Square?

*The first thing that attracts Heads to Round Square is that it is an **international** body — and is so in unique ways. Exchanges to other countries are especially attractive, and Round Square is a secure and effective tool for making these happen. Staff interactions are also attractive (actual teacher exchanges have been a frustrating issue to bring about, but are still important and worth pursuing.)*

What are the most important products of the relationship?

Service! Service is one of the greatest things we've done together, and a central part of Round Square; and we were part of the process from the beginning.

What challenges lie ahead for Round Square in India?

I think there are three: how schools in this country (and some others) connect to Round Square at the Board level, how we lead and support ourselves as a region, and how Regional Membership is really going to work, in practical terms. All these "challenges" have been produced by Round Square's growth and success here and elsewhere — but that doesn't mean they don't have to be solved.

§

The striking similarity about the three schools we have just glimpsed is that, in each case, the school is substantially older than Round Square, and each developed its own version of the "IDEALS" without either Round Square or (as far as I have been able to determine) the "Hahn schools" as a model.

Each therefore came to this alliance of peer schools with its own Round Square-type vision in place, and thus with much to give as well as something which through the alliance each school hoped to gain. Each went on to find that the international context provided by Round Square has not only added new perspectives, but stimulated the further development of its own home-grown approach to the "IDEALS."

Later in this book we will look at some of the currents of thought which have influenced the thinking of those who developed the programs of the Round Square schools. But, for now, it may be sufficient to say the following about the motives and goals of these three schools:

- In each case, the school defined its objectives in terms which went well beyond the traditional goals of most secondary schools. Furthermore, the expansion of mission in each school relates to the pursuit of long-term, *behavioral* objectives, such as "character," "leadership" and "social usefulness."
- Each has pursued a strategic vision which is rooted less in educational theory or the conferring of a competitive advantage for university-bound youngsters than in a sense of having a duty to prepare students to "make the difference" during a time of emerging national identity.
- In all three schools, there is a common thread of trying to *prepare individual young people* (to cite part of St. Cyprian's motto), *"not for school, but for life."*
- And in each, there is an acknowledgement that the pursuit of the Round Square "IDEALS" provides not just positive benefits, but a force which diminishes the elitist attitudes which can attend an outstanding school's excellence.

It was precisely this last and most undesirable side-effect of receiving an superior education which Archbishop Tutu was referencing when he described St. Cyprian's as providing "excellence without elitism."

One of the most common — and valid — criticisms made of selective and / or unusually ambitious schools such as these (and, in fact, of all Round Square schools) is that, wherever in the world they may be located, they have a potential to promote a feeling of entitlement or elitism in their students which undermines the egalitarian spirit that any effective democracy requires, and especially in its leaders.

Elitism is or should be a concern for all schools whose students are expected to aspire to and perform at levels which their national societies consider "excellent." The issue is the same whether a school is operated by a government, a private or non-profit entity, or a religious organization. It is the same whether attendance is controlled by selective admissions, an "open" but scores-driven admissions-testing process, or geographic "districting" which restricts enrollment to children of families from a privileged neighborhood. All these mechanisms enable a top-quality school to attain, and confer, elite status. When this elite status is not effectively challenged and countered through the experience of each youngster, then the school's status will be perceived by students as a *professed value system*. That is what we mean by *elitism*.

The social circumstances in suburban Canada, central Cape Town, or a foothills city in India are different. However, the potentially harmful outcome for the larger societies in each country if its best schools are allowed to become engines of elitism will be the same.

Round Square is proving to be a useful source of anti-elitist leverage for schools which aspire to perform at the highest levels, but at the same time want to produce the best kind of leaders for their nations — young people whose usefulness is *not* undermined by elitism.

The students should have the last word on this topic:

> *{Recently} I participated in a social service project in the village of Chemdy, in Ladakh. To tell you the truth, the whole experience was wonderful. It wasn't just one event which had a profound impact on me. For instance, the interchanges between those of us who were from India and the other global citizens who worked with us kept showing how similar we all were; it was almost as if we'd agreed in advance with each other! This is probably due to the technologically advanced conditions we all*

live in. However, the villagers, whose lives are rough and extreme, were a surprise to all of us — despite this lack of sophistication and their simplicity, they really impressed us all. The whole Ladakh experience widened my scope of knowledge, and boosted my confidence. — Male student, India

The most important thing I learned during my project was the fact that the so-called job of "unskilled labor" requires a lot of skill. It was surprising to see the ease with which the local workers did their jobs while the Round Square students struggled. — Male student, India

Chapter 5:
Improving the World, One Student at a Time

MOST ROUND SQUARE SCHOOLS developed their present aims and objectives during the twentieth century. Yet, similar as these aims and objectives seem to be, the schools were at great distances from each other, geographically and culturally. Only a few of those who shaped the direction of the institutions can be shown to have had a direct connection to, or an awareness of, one another. Many acted utterly alone.

Remarkably, these collaborating schools exhibit great differences in structure and makeup. Their objectives may be similar, but their formats are not. Moreover, there is little evidence that any of the schools feels compelled by the alliance, however powerfully invested in it they may be, to reduce school-to-school differences.

Certainly, the emergence of a "community of like-minded schools" around the world, something which (if we leave aside denominational school systems) appears to be unprecedented, cannot be seen as a mere coincidence. For this reason alone, Round Square proposes questions which merit a response. Specifically: *How* did the ideas, principles and objectives which brought these schools together arise? *Why* did that development happen when it did? And *why* is Round Square flourishing now?

§

A glance over the "life stories" of the Round Square schools in search of common patterns offers one way to start our search for what brought these institutions together. Some commonalties are immediately obvious:

- All Round Square schools are *independently governed*. These are schools relatively free from higher-level direction of program and policy. They can frame their own missions, determine their own curricula, initiate programs, and choose leaders as they see fit. They are also more accountable for educational outcomes to students and parents than to bureaucracies or legislative bodies.
- All are *"schools of choice."* Students who attend Round Square schools *elect* to do so. And the schools are able to admit only those candidates who seem suitable for the kind of education being offered.

- While these are strong schools, most are *twentieth-century foundations* — so, in many countries, they would be seen as "young." Even in cases where schools were founded before 1900, one can usually identify a period of transformation (often led by a visionary head of school) during the twentieth century which shaped today's institution.
- Within their own countries, Round Square schools are *not likely to be viewed as "alternative," "experimental" or "radical."* Most would be described as "academically excellent" and most send graduates to top-ranked universities. In fact, many are best known and respected for these "conventional" kinds of high achievement. And they aren't obscure; many would be described by the media as "prestigious."
- Most remarkable, perhaps, is *that virtually none of these schools has been shaped or led by an educational "expert" or reformer*. Rather, the Round Square schools are the creations of pragmatists. A good many of the leaders and founders have not only been averse to theorizing, but many might not even have been seen as qualified to do so. In fact, when we look closely, we find that the majority of those who gave Round Square schools their current forms were not trained to be educators. A surprising number never even took a university degree.

For example, the man who would not agree to be seen as Round Square's guiding spirit, Kurt Hahn, studied at no less than five universities, but never graduated from any of them (his Doctorate was honorary). All his experience and training prior to becoming the Headmaster of Salem was as a civil servant. Starehe's Geoffrey Griffin never attended a university at all. He told me that the most useful preparation for school leadership which he had received had nothing to do with educational institutions *per se*, but was the officer training course to which the Colonial army had sent him at the beginning of the Mau Mau war. Round Square's Founder Director, Jocelin Winthrop Young, headed two schools and nurtured the organization through its initial decades, but never attended a university or had any formal training as an educational professional. His education after Salem and Gordonstoun related to his service as an officer in the Royal Navy or as a Foreign Service officer. Gulab Ramchandani, one of the great shapers of Doon School and a leading factor in the formation of the Round Square International Service, came to Doon directly from a successful career as a business executive (Doon's governors knew they needed a skilled manager at that moment, and felt that, as a Doon graduate, Ramchandani would know enough about the school to figure out the educational details on the job...which he did). Dyke Brown of Athenian had been a foundation executive, not an educator, before he became a founding Headmaster. And Frank Boyden of Deerfield moved directly from obtaining a BA at Amherst College to become, at age 22, Headmaster of Deerfield. He had no training for such a position, and he had no intention of remaining at Deerfield one day longer than it would take to save the money he'd need for law school.

What these leaders shared was not just their common status as professional "outsiders." With the exception of Boyden, all came to this work with practical leadership and management experience in the non-educational world. They shared a profound interest in the development of young people, but it was an interest unfettered by the assumptions fostered by training and certification processes common to the educational profession.

Well into his fifth decade at Deerfield, Boyden remarked:

I have just gone ahead from day to day without any particular theory or any particular policy except a real personal interest in the boys, in their work, and in their activities.

Of course, Boyden's disclaimer notwithstanding, this actually is a statement of "theory" and "policy." It just isn't a statement which one can file away in an intellectually familiar ("particular") way.

For Boyden, education started with each individual human being who had been placed in his care. Boyden's intention was to achieve a direct understanding of each young person. Obviously, this was an approach which was fundamentally based on the observation of *behavior*. It was focused on what a young person *does* — on "work" and "activities." He professed his school's aims this way:

*{A} thorough grounding not only in basic academics but, **almost more important**, in training...attitudes toward life which will persist long after the precise details of book-training have dimmed.* [emphasis mine].

§

All of those who created today's Round Square schools and framed Round Square as an organization led lives shaped by the first half of the twentieth century. How might that era have influenced their thinking and helped align their views and their goals?

Certainly as the century began, and then progressed, *any* thinking person would have been aware that profound changes were taking place in the ways in which both society and individual human beings were being considered. Even if one had never read the writings of the more revolutionary shapers of the era's intellectual history, such as Darwin, Marx, Freud, Fraser, William James, and Dewey, the general world of ideas, whether expressed in academia or the mass media, was being formed in response to each of them.

In particular, the era witnessed a new willingness to view man and society in ways which related more closely to the emerging social sciences than to the old ways of academic philosophy and theology. Man's nature was being re-defined as something less innate and universal than had previously been thought. What was emerging in the place of this old way of thinking was a view of the individual as an empirically-developed construct. Each person was being seen as a unique creation, substantially shaped by what that individual had experienced, singly and in the context of family, society and culture, from birth onward.

With such a change in thinking underway in learned circles and in the media, it is not surprising that some of those involved in education (not only its practitioners, but its "customers") began to think about education in new ways. This development led a number of individuals to place less value in the traditional view of schooling as a transfer of knowledge and skills. Instead, they were exploring how one might direct or "co-opt" the shaping of attitudes and character through the careful organization of a student's outside-the-classroom activities and experiences. In such a view, "curriculum" would now be seen not so much in the narrow sense of "course content," but as an *empirical design*. This design would lead a child into activities and experiences which, if appropriately promoted and supported by educators, were likely to have meaningful and abiding results.

It was becoming difficult to sustain a view of education as a didactic enterprise, the so-called "old wine into new bottles" undertaking. How the particular *bottle* could be formed now seemed to be at least as important a determiner of long-term outcomes as the particulars of the *wine* to be inserted. If that were so, then a logical next question had to follow: if experience shaped both character and enduring attitudes, and if these traits determined so much about what a person might accomplish in life, then why not focus more of a school's energy on the shaping of experience?

As he commanded his teachers to "impel [students] into experience," Kurt Hahn explained precisely this view of curriculum:

> *Every girl and boy has a "grande passion," often hidden and unrealized to the end of life. The educator cannot hope and may not try to find it out by psycho-analytical methods. It can and will be revealed by the child coming into close touch with a number of different activities...but these activities must not be added as a superstructure to an exhausting program of lessons. They will have no chance of absorbing and bringing out the child unless they form a vital part of the day's work.*

Hahn was inclined to deflect other questions about philosophy and method. As Martin Flavin recounts in his book *Kurt Hahn's Schools and Legacy*:

> *Hahn had no "theory" of education, and considered originality to be as out of place in education as in medicine. He often quoted Prince Max's reply to an "over-enthusiastic" American visitor's question about what he was most proud of in the school: "There is nothing original. That is what I am most proud of. We have stolen from everywhere."*

Here again, a seemingly humble disclaimer should not be taken at face value. Those who, in developing their school, had "stolen from everywhere" obviously performed their thievery in a way which was shaped by an abiding purpose. Hahn's professed lack of "theory" really reflected a re-ordering of priorities, within which no abstract "theory" could come first. Rather, the *potential within each individual student* came first. That's the message in the motto of Hahn's second school, Gordonstoun (*Plus est en Vous*, or, there's more in you than you think). It's the educator's job to help the individual student discover what the proposed "more" really is. That revelation starts by "impelling" the student into experience.

How does one actually "impel" students in ways which will lead them to self-discovery? One example might be the unique adventure-canoeing program developed during the first third of the 20th century at Lakefield College School in Canada, under the leadership of Alex Mackenzie. While Mackenzie's long tenure as Headmaster ended before Round Square began, it surprised no one when the unusual, adventure-enriched school which he had shaped became the first Canadian Round Square member. Having departed long since from the trodden path and seen what that could do for young people, Lakefield was more than ready to join hands with others who were moving in a similar direction.

Thus it happened that, within the general public and in at least some corners of academia, old verities and old methods were losing some of their respectability, when examined in the cool light of new ways of thinking. The spirit of the time was causing those concerned with schools to look much more critically at how well, or badly, the traditional model of schooling was serving young people and the world.

In Australia, a headmaster who had a direct and powerful influence on many leaders of today's Round Square schools, J. R. Darling, Headmaster of Geelong Grammar School from 1930 to 1961, put it this way:

Schoolmasters of my day were becoming increasingly conscious of the sterility...of the twin gods of scholarship and athleticism as a sufficient basis for a good school. These values neglected too many...who were neither scholars not athletes. Furthermore, they tended, unless one was very careful, to divide the school into two parts — the worshippers of rival gods; and they left a large portion of man's potential undeveloped altogether, and even militated against its development.

This kind of thinking ultimately led Darling to found the influential Timbertop program as an integral part of his school's educational design. This innovation resulted in each Geelong student's being sent for a year at about the age of fourteen to live, be taught, and work collaboratively with peers — and, while there, to live rough — at the rustic Timbertop campus, which was deep in the mountainous back country of Victoria. Although Darling cited a variety of influences, including that of Hahn and of his experience at Repton in England under William Temple, as sources of the ideas which formed Timbertop, he also noted that the ideas were as much homegrown as borrowed.

In his view, Timbertop was a natural outgrowth of the "national service" program which had flourished at Geelong since the 1930's, and which was a powerful part of the school's culture. Darling was also aware that at least two other Australian schools were trying to give students a taste of non-urban living through back-country "forestry camps." He saw this as a "revolt against the urbanization" of Australia. And then there was "the deeper psychological theory" that living at Timbertop could provide specific positive experiences (and forestall some less desirable ones) which might help young people "develop independence and self-confidence" and cope more effectively with the stresses of early adolescence.

But, as he cited these influences, Darling went on as follows:

The truth is that ideas do not proceed in a direct genealogical tree from an original thinker to a number of inheritors, but rather do they arise in more or less similar forms at the same time, as a result of a need being gradually recognized.

This statement could serve as the epigraph to this entire chapter. *Sometimes there is not a single seed idea, or "seminal thinker" behind a wave of innovation.* Rather, it may be that a new kind of *need* powerfully announces itself, and everything starts with a growing recognition of this need. At times, needs which must be addressed are local and particular. But, now and then, these needs may be general — even global.

We should take Darling's hint, and be aware of the fallacy in assuming that there *must* be a direct transmission of thought when new ideas seem to arise simultaneously. Similar kinds of thinking about the *needs which had to be addressed* by those concerned with the education and training of young people were occurring within schools and beyond them, around the world. While it is the specific purpose of this book to look at one type of response to these perceived needs, innovations in *non*-school-based strategies were also happening during the first half of the century. These, of course, included the spread of scouting (Boy and Girl Scouts / Guides) and, in many countries, the "camping movement." Those developments were widespread and popular, and can certainly be seen as significant concurring events.

It is probable that school-based efforts to expand curriculum to embrace each young person's experience were not only being energized but most likely given credibility by these parallel developments. All provided evidence of a broadly perceived *need.* It is also demonstrable that, at its most fundamental level, pre-university education has always been more susceptible to utilitarian adaptation in response to evolving social needs than many educational historians have wanted to admit.

Bernard Bailyn's brilliant *Education in the Forming of American Society* (Norton, New York, 1972) is a penetrating analysis of the "response-to-need" process. Bailyn presents a situation where one society's perception of a changing need in what young people must be able to do when they become adult, a need which cannot be met by family, church, or community, drove a change in the expectations which colonial-era American society came to hold for its schools.

What might have caused a perception of a new type of need to arise in the twentieth century? What caused it to gain sufficient attention that it was able to spark such widespread examples of innovation in the education and training of the young? In a memoir about Hahn written during the 1970's, Olivia Campbell, a history teacher and one of the original members of the Gordonstoun School staff, expressed the need which had motivated Hahn as he formed Salem in this manner:

> *At Salem Hahn quite clearly set himself to break the German habit of obedience to authority, and he demanded that those at Salem should accept personal responsibility and should obey their conscience...his moves to weaken class distinctions and narrow nationalism no doubt helped to create a new Germany after the war.*

As an aide to Germany's Chancellor during World War I, Hahn had certainly seen all too vividly the cost of his nation's "habit of obedience." This "habit" clearly was a determining factor not only in Germany's willingness to follow its leaders into deeper and deeper tragedy long after the war's hopelessness had become evident, but in the unwillingness of the leadership cadre itself to stand up against those who were at the top of their hierarchy and whose judgment was wrong.

Moreover, Hahn had surely seen that much the same problem had been evident during the war years in Britain, where he had spent much of his young manhood. Britain's leaders had also been unable to avert the war, and they seemed just as unable to escape the years of bloody, futile slaughter which developed when the war ground to a stalemate.

It seemed self-evident to him that the fates of nations could hang on the abilities of the foremost schools, places where future leaders were likely to be trained, to instill *different personal qualities* in those they were educating from those which had been taught to the prior generation:

> *He realized that...an education was required that would develop a less class-divided society and one where {students} would learn to be responsible, independent, interested and compassionate.*

What is most striking about these goals is, first, that they have almost nothing to do with what were then seen as the "traditional" objectives of schooling. Second, it is evident that the need driving these objectives was not the betterment of education in an ordinary sense, but the transformation of institutional education for the betterment of society. Indeed, as Campbell remarked:

> *Hahn never thought only of Gordonstoun but kept thinking of people and nations and how he set out to affect their thinking, to build men who would take responsibility for their country and encourage honesty, unselfishness, compassion and determination.*

The *need* which the war had taught Hahn about was not just relevant to the training of those who might hold national leadership in a time of crisis, but to the shaping of the attitudes and characters of all those who would influence the construction and maintenance of democracies — for the same war had also made it clear that the leaders of the future were less likely to be determined by members of a stable, elite class, and far more likely to emerge through the workings (for good or ill) of democracies.

How then might the attitudes and traits which could underpin the leaders of a successful, stable democracy be formed? Again, Hahn turned to the instructional power of experience:

> *Even the youngsters ought to undertake tasks which are of definite importance for the community. Tell them from the start, you want a crew, not passengers...Let the responsible boys and girls shoulder duties big enough, when negligently performed, to wreck a state.*

His objective, then, as it was for a scattering of other innovators around the world, included training for democracy via the experience of having and using democratic responsibility as a part of one's schooling.

Across the Atlantic, Frank Boyden was reaching similar conclusions about how to educate in a way which could lead to an effective democracy:

> *Let the people make their own mistakes. Let them come into knowledge and understanding by their experience. Little progress can be made by merely repressing what is evil. Our great hope lies in developing what is good.*

Years later, Geoffrey Griffin, for whom the personal experience of war had also been galvanizing, and who was determined to build a school at Starehe which could help Kenya become an effective democracy, was finding his own way to many of the same conclusions about how to meet a changing social need:

> *It IS possible to run a school by methods contrary to those generally accepted...by giving pupils considerable freedom of movement and speech; by training them to handle major responsibilities in the administration of their school; by bringing them, without force, to reject bullying within the school and to joyfully accept community service outside it; by enabling them to follow a wide range of co-curricular activities without prejudice to academic work, and, generally, by creating an environment in which discipline and punishment are NOT synonymous terms.*

Professional educators tend to approach the subject of how schooling might be improved only after a number of *a priori* assumptions are made. The first of these is usually that all accepted notions about the main *purpose* of schooling will not be on the table. Thus absolved from any reason to embark on a reform of education in a *strategic* context, they proceed to debate what are, at best, proposals for *tactical* improvement of an enterprise which may, in fact, be more in need of a deep strategic revision than of incremental improvement.

Those who put Round Square and its member schools on their strategically distinctive courses felt no such *a priori* inhibitions as they set about their work. This was in part the result of their having in so many cases been without conventional educational training. However, it's far more significant that the energizing factor in their initiatives was not to develop a better school, but to *build a better society*. The methods they developed were pragmatic and experimental. In most cases, the approaches which produced success — and were retained — were those which were rooted in education through experience.

The social needs to be addressed by each school usually were expressed by school leaders as being particular to the national and historic situation in which each school found itself. In post-revolutionary Kenya, for instance, an excessive inclination to obey authority was *not* a major problem; but Griffin and his colleagues realized that one of the great challenges his country and many other African ex-colonies would have to face was that of corruption. Griffin saw both the roots of this problem — and its potential solution — in how Kenya's schools were run:

> *Let us consider for a moment what lessons a leaver from {a typical Kenyan school} will carry away with him.*
>
> *He will have gained a fair bounty of academic knowledge — the school is quite competent in that respect. But the lesson in which he had been thoroughly indoctrinated is that might is right: that the law of the land can be openly flouted, and dishonesty be practiced, by someone who attains a position of sufficient power…since many of our schools have been teaching this sort of lesson in one way or another for decades, it is perhaps not too surprising that dishonesty and corruption is…so widespread in our country.*

Starehe's program was meant to lead in a different direction altogether, and thereby to lead Kenya itself. In time, there was startling proof that it was doing so:

> *During the 1991 examinations for the Kenya Certificate of Secondary Education, half-a-dozen of our boys were stunned to realize that the paper before them was word-for-word the same as a "practice test" borrowed from pupils in another school. Emerging from the examination hall, they came together and took only minutes to decide that, although it was likely to be to their detriment and might be to their danger, the only right course of action was to report the matter to me — which they did, and, in turn, I passed the information to the Examinations Council. The leakage eventually proved to be so widespread in Nairobi and other parts of the country that the entire examination had to be suspended…Starehe was the only school that reported it — and it was from our report alone that the Police traced it back to its source among the Council's employees. The moral courage that our boys had shown made us very proud.*

In his decision to tell this story, his manner of telling it, and most explicitly the anecdote's last sentence, Griffin was leading his readers (and his students) to one of the greatest, and least understood, central truths about the kind of education he and his Round Square peers were undertaking. That is that the tap root for this form of instruction absolutely *must* find as its source the educator's real respect and concern for each young person who is involved. This must not only involve a respect for the *potential of each student to make a difference in the world*, but a *willingness to let the student embark on making a difference **now***, and to *talk about and celebrate* events which confirm the validity of this attitude.

As Griffin or the others who shaped Round Square and its schools saw it, the educator's transaction with each student is not a conventionally formal or didactic one. Rather, it is felt by youngsters as an "I — Thou" bond. An alliance based on two-way respect and trust is the basis. The adult expresses respect and trust in the risk he takes by empowering the student. The student expresses respect in taking this empowerment seriously, and trust by assuming that the adult knows the student may fail, and can be counted on to help the student preserve self-respect while learning from failure. As the following chapter shows, Round Square students agree that the outcome of one's involvement in Round Square is not to be found in experiences themselves, but in the discoveries these experiences promote.

Students often talk about how a Round Square project or exchange will require them to "get out of the comfort zone." However, this kind of educational approach also takes adults who are responsibly involved out of *their* comfort zones. It takes courage for a youngster to go off alone to live at a school in another country for a term, spend a vacation doing hard work in a third world environment, or through such ventures to confront massive differences of values and culture. It also takes courage for a student to hang on to his or her own deepest beliefs and conscience when faced with contrary expectations. But Round Square requires courage in *adults*, too, due to the challenges they must face in order to support young people who are learning in this manner.

A commitment to this kind of education inevitably leads the educator to understand his or her relationship to the student in a way that is *different*. Certainly, professional clarity about roles and boundaries must still be present, and this merits careful monitoring. However, the demand for personal integrity which is being presented to the student can create situations which challenge the adult as well.

Perhaps the best example of what this sense of one's personal responsibility as an educational leader may require was Hahn's reaction to the takeover of Germany by the Nazi party. During World War I, he and his future Board chair at Salem, Prince Max, opposed government war policy, but when their advice was over-ruled, they loyally stayed on. However, in 1932, when Hitler demanded that five Nazi storm troopers who had just been convicted of murdering a young Communist be set free ("your freedom," Hitler telegraphed to them, "is our honor"), Hahn the educator wrote to all Salem graduates to announce that "Salem cannot remain neutral." He asked each graduate to either "break with Salem or with Hitler." Soon thereafter, having heard claims that the programs of the Hitler Youth were being described as no different than Salem's training of its students through leadership, service, and adventure, Hahn stepped in front of a public audience and flatly rebutted such a view. Something crucial was missing in the Nazi program for the young, he said, and its absence made all the difference. What the Hitler Youth failed to offer young people was "the power of carrying out what is recognized to be *just*." Without a primary regard for justice and without compassion, Hahn said, the program would be worse than worthless. "We *need* to be able to feel that as a people we are just and kindly," he concluded.

Hahn the public servant might have accepted defeat, but Hahn the educator could not be silent. He had to act as he had long advocated his students should. That he did so at grave peril, not only because of his views but because he was Jewish, and that he was jailed soon after by the Nazi government, must have surprised no one, Hahn included. That he survived, escaped from Germany, and lived to found another school (and more) was what was astonishing.

§

So many roots, influences and trends! Is there a way to sum up the factors that caused Round Square to emerge when and as it did? Perhaps turning back once again to the relief project in Greece in 1954 offers one way to do so.

That project brought together students and adults from like-minded schools in three European countries. All those who proposed and led the project had already developed a belief in the power of service learning. But none had yet seen its full potential, particularly if the service experience might occur in a multi-school, international context.

The project occurred in the wake of World War II, before the present European community had been developed, but when the ideas which would lead to it were already very much in play. The adults who were involved had all come to their educational roles in unconventional ways. They were not beholden to a professional culture which might have inhibited the imaginations of their peers. All had substantial experience with leading young people — although, for many of them, this had been a result of leadership in war, not in schools.

Each had come to maturity in the first half of the twentieth century, and was thus the heir of its revolutionary trends in thinking. Each was old enough to be aware of the era's failures, and to be keenly aware of the dangers their societies were facing. International institutions and, to an extent, democracy, had failed to prevent the cataclysm of the last war. Could such institutions be trusted to do any better now? It was clear that a different and no less complex or dangerous world would have to be dealt with by the next generation of young people. But if the next generation were to do better as leaders, they would need to be able to reach more confidently, knowledgeably, and compassionately beyond the narrow boundaries of nationality, self-interest, and the arrogance of power than had been the case in the past. They would need an extraordinary range of skills and courage, a sophisticated vision of the world, and real moral fiber if they were to guide the planet toward a better destiny.

Clearly a shared realization of "need" animated these observers. But the need was not "educational reform" in any usual sense of that term. Not one of the surviving founders has related anything which suggests that he was thinking about a way to improve *schools*. On the contrary, virtually all the evidence I gathered via interviews with the individuals who survive and which exists in archival materials is focused not on the nature of schooling, but on its long-term social objective.

Round Square's founders were *driven by a need to improve the world*.

The engagement of the students in Cephalonia suggested to the adult leaders that a means might exist to make a difference in meeting this global "need" — if similar undertakings were to occur repeatedly and if they involved enough countries and enough schools dedicated to producing intellectual and social leaders. They had experienced a leap of understanding during that summer. What they had seen in and through those young people had suggested how transformative such an experience could be, *for students,* and how powerful it might become in meeting a larger world need.

So attuned by their own era and by the kind of education they had themselves experienced, this leap of understanding was not in fact a huge one for them — as far as it went. But the rest of the picture remained incomplete. While they grasped the implications of what they saw happening, they were not prepared to imagine how they might institutionalize a multi-school, international experience as a part of the regular conduct of schooling. They had no notion about what Round Square would have to develop, through trial and error, over the next fifty years. They really did not grasp how a larger grouping of schools such as theirs might be assembled, and its collaborative machinery be developed, to make this kind of educational experience happen, again and again, around the world, not just for a hundred students from three European schools, but for thousands of youngsters from countries everywhere.

Yet *something* had begun — not yet an organization or even a plan. What should such a development be called? In their book about Outward Bound, Josh Miner and Joe Boldt remark that:

> *While each {Outward Bound} school is a big story in itself, deserving of its own book, the movement is **the** big story.*

Much the same might be said about Round Square. *The movement is the big story.* The project in Greece began a *movement*. The general tenor of the time and the particular life histories of those who were on the scene prepared them to be deeply stirred by that experience, and to emerge as the movement's leaders. What happened then? An organization began to support this movement during the years that followed.

When Hahn prohibited the founders of Round Square to name itself after him, advising them as he did so that other school leaders in the world were surely doing many of the same things which he had developed at his own schools, he was not only guessing accurately, but had to be aware that the social needs which had so deeply motivated him and the other educators were by no means restricted to a few countries. Others would inevitably be trying to meet similar needs in similar ways, without any connection with him. Nothing should be allowed to be done which might inhibit the future fellowship of such schools with those whose leaders were meeting with him at Gordonstoun.

We've noted a number of the intellectual and social forces which shaped and "seeded" Round Square. However, in 1966-67, the Cold War was in high gear, the colonial era was collapsing, and a climate of support for truly international institutions was in its infancy. Consider too that "independent" schools such as those which made up Round Square when it began and continue to make up its membership are not given that name lightly. They may have freedom to innovate, but they are notoriously resistant to relationships which might limit their freedom to set unique objectives and employ their own ideas and methods. A durable international consortium of like-minded independent schools, all of which would bind themselves to cooperate with and influence each other, share in the education of each other's students, and collaborate democratically in the operation of a coordinating structure, not only was without precedent, it had to be developed in spite of powerful counterforces. One by one, these obstacles were confronted and overcome. And thus the organization driven by the Round Square movement endured, expanded, gained widespread respect, and now flourishes. Currently Round Square is present on every continent, and is an energizing force in scores of the world's outstanding schools. Round Square will certainly continue to change, but by now it seems to be here to stay.

Is there a unique message which Round Square has to relate to educators around the world? That message may be less concerned with Round Square's own ideals and programs, important and worthy as they may be, than it is a message vested in Round Square's endurance, persistent growth and increasing stature as a *movement*. The development of an international *movement* which substantially challenges and thereby aids involved schools and their students, while at the same time remaining flexible and relatively unconstraining of invention and creativity, is no longer an idea without precedent or credibility. It's *here*. It has endured. And it works.

New ideas and new realities continue to develop and affect Round Square, just as new generations are arriving in its schools. We have already seen how the emergence of environmental concerns drove a substantial change in Round Square's mission and programs during the last two decades of the twentieth century. Currently, the most salient new forces which are on the scene include the "trans-national" view of information and ideas which has accompanied the Internet's proliferation (few educational organizations have more readily or productively made use of this resource), and a similar "world is flat" vision of the future that the rapid globalization of world commerce and finance encourages. Exactly how these new currents of thought and ways of living will affect Round Square in the decades to come is as yet unclear. That they are driving and will continue to drive change is nevertheless obvious.

And so, shaped as it was by the ideas and needs of the twentieth century, Round Square remains a work in progress, while it has become something of an icon — an influential "new idea" — for those living in the twenty-first century.

Chapter Six:
Students and Graduates Assess Round Square

> *I left my life in Australia and came to South Africa to live with a totally new group of people...{this helped me} realize that there is more to the world than just my own life and a few others around me. Although there are six billion humans on earth, we are all really the same, whether we are rich, poor, European, American, Asian, African, Christian, Muslim, Hindu, or Jewish...all of this {understanding} would have been impossible without my school's being a member of Round Square. The exchange experience opened my eyes to a **wide** world.*
> — Female student, Australia

DURING LATE 2004 AND EARLY 2005, I conducted a six-month inquiry that examined Round Square students' and graduates' attitudes about their experience. There were two basic parts of this study: a widely distributed, anonymous questionnaire (see Appendix D), which could be submitted by any student or graduate of a Round Square school; and a series of group interviews, conducted at seventeen schools in Australia, Canada, Germany, India, Kenya, South Africa, the United Kingdom, and the United States. The particular schools chosen for interviews were selected to provide a mixture of institutional types, a range of nationalities, and differences in the number of years of Round Square membership.

The interviews were not only valuable from a research point of view, but were utterly fascinating. Candidly, I would have *loved* to have been able to spend more time talking with students and graduates, at more schools. However, constraints of time and funding demanded that choices be made.

The questionnaires were designed to produce both statistical data and personal anecdotes (excerpts from which are used throughout this book). On-campus group interviews with students and graduates were conducted in a uniform manner, to yield *comparable* responses, although their smaller populations and the discussion methodology limited the potential for statistical analysis. Individual interviews with Heads, Round Square Reps, a few school Governors, and Round Square leaders past and present were very helpful, but were not structured to produce comparable data.

More than 900 students and graduates in thirteen countries

submitted questionnaires. About three hundred students and graduates as well as sixty school leaders and staff took part in on-site interviews. Those who were interviewed are acknowledged by name (see Appendix C). There is, of course, no way to identify the persons who submitted anonymous questionnaires. However, I want to assure each of those who did so that he or she made a real contribution to this project, and I am deeply grateful for this assistance.

During the period when I was traveling from school to school to interview students, graduates, staff and administrators, I not only made notes of all conversations, but kept a journal of observations and reflections. The interview notes and my journal, as well as more formal research findings, were sources for what follows.

§

The student / graduate questionnaire was meant to meet three main objectives:

• Get feedback from the young people Round Square serves concerning the *degree to which their views reflect values and attitudes which Round Square hopes to instill.*
• Gather *comments about individual experiences* of Round Square activities, and the individual's sense of what was learned.
• Gain insight about *whether a young person's involvement with Round Square is likely to promote — or inhibit — elitism.*

The ten questions in Part I were (with one exception) developed by simply re-phrasing segments of Round Square's stated objectives. My intention was to measure students' and graduates' agreement or disagreement with Round Square's main goals.

The exception was the fifth question — "Being well educated makes a person more valuable to the world than other people" —which was in *no* way derived from Round Square's aims. It was meant to gauge whether a student would break the predicted positive answering pattern in order to register *disagreement* with a statement which, as written, could be seen as an expression of elitism.

Responses poured in! Regrettably, on-line filing was beyond the skill level of some who replied, and other respondents were apparently so unfamiliar with the "one to seven, agree / disagree" type of opinion survey that they were confused by it. For these reasons, approximately 40 submissions had to be discarded as "spoiled." Happily, this was a small percentage of those received. I was able to use surveys filed by 863 students and graduates (466 males, 397 females) from nine countries. This total exceeded expectations.

The number of surveys per country and region was reasonably reflective of the Round Square community. Canada and the U.K. overachieved slightly, while responses from Australia and India were relatively lean in relation to student / graduate numbers. However, these variations were not great enough to impair the reliability of the data.

§

Statistical analysis of the surveys provided information which was profoundly illuminating. The most important finding related to the degree to which students and graduates endorsed attitudes and values that reflect Round Square's fundamental objectives. Respondents *agreed to a highly significant degree with every one of the questions* that tested attitudes toward the nine statements which were, in fact, re-wordings of Round Square's explicit goals. The message could not have been clearer. **Round Square's educational strategy works**, *if the desired result is agreement with Round Square's professed values by students and graduates of member schools.*

There was variance only in the *strength* of agreement. The two strongest areas of concurrence were with the second and sixth questions: "If my generation does the right things, we CAN provide a better life for the world's people" and, "Every human being has a responsibility for the protection of the global environment." In contrast, responses to two other questions, while still highly positive, were a bit less powerful. These were the seventh and tenth questions: "I believe it is important for all of us to think of ourselves as citizens of the world, not merely as citizens of our own nations" and, "I now know that I can accomplish much more with my life than I had once thought possible". The relative difference may invite speculation, but it must be emphasized that the differences are merely matters of degree within a group of overwhelmingly positive responses. The response pattern as a whole provides striking evidence that *the individual students at Round Square schools "buy into" the ideals which the organization professes.*

The fifth question in Part I — *"Being well educated makes a person more valuable to the world than other people"* — was, in one Canadian student's wry words, "the joker in the deck." That remark reflected a bright youngster's awareness that something different was going on here. He was correct. Not only would a positive response to this question reflect *nothing* contained in Round Square's objectives, but it would concur with a statement expressing elitism. Such an attitude, while not explicitly addressed by Round Square's founders, is nevertheless one that must be seen as counter to their fundamental intentions.

When the questionnaires were assessed, the mean *response to this question — and this alone — was negative*. While the significance factor (p= .10) was not strong enough to say that "no matter how such a question is asked, the same population would always disagree to the same degree," the contrast between participants' negative responses and their positive reactions to all other questions make the difference highly significant.

It is clear that *Round Square's students and alumni will oppose a statement which expresses elitism*. This finding suggests that the one of the key (even if not explicitly voiced) ambitions which motivated Round Square's founders is being fulfilled by today's schools.

Part II asks students to "describe one specific experience you had as a result of a Round Square program or activity." It was assumed that students / graduates who had significant and memorable personal experiences through Round Square would be likely to offer a comment. (Of course, there is no way to know if no comment indicated a *lack* of a significant Round Square experience.) It was also reasonable to guess that students who had something to say in Part II would be more inclined to positively value Round Square. The latter assumption proved true. *A significantly more positive response to all questions (except the fifth) correlated with the inclusion of a written comment in Part II.*

But while the responses of a person who wrote a comment were apt to be more positive, the over-all pattern of response to the questions discussed above remained the same. *One may therefore conclude that an increase in experience increases the intensity of feeling, but not the over-all pattern of agreement.*

Although a slightly larger number of males filed questionnaires than did females, a larger percentage of females added comments in Part II than did males. One might theorize about the reasons for this discrepancy — are more girls than boys currently going on exchanges, service projects, or expeditions, or attending conferences? Are girls simply more willing to talk about personal experiences? No conclusive answer is possible. What must be said, though, is that because writing a comment correlated with a more positive pattern of response, and because girls were somewhat more likely to submit a comment, the average female ended up ranking all items except the fifth question slightly more positively than the average male.

This gender pattern was not consistent from country to country. However, when I attempted to compare sub-groupings (by gender, nation, student / graduate, age group, etc.), I almost always found myself dealing with unreliable findings because these analyses were all based on sub-segments of the total population which were not large enough to provide statistical reliability. It therefore seems prudent to step past all these detailed questions and simply say that *the responses which have been discussed are reliable and significant for the Round Square population as a whole and probably* predict that similar patterns will be exhibited by other Round Square schools or regional groups within Round Square if a larger study is conducted.

Finally, *the graduates' responses did not look much different than the student ones*. Again, we need to be cautious, since the graduate population was smaller than the student one. However, the *pattern* of graduate responses closely resembled findings concerning student attitudes and values. They were highly positive about all of Round Square's value propositions, and negative regarding elitism. So it is fair to say that these findings *probably* indicate that attitudes exhibited by students persist well after these young people have left Round Square schools. That assumption is reinforced by findings obtained through group interviews.

§

*Alice Springs, Australia: Session today with recent graduates. Advice (again!) — "make sure people know it's **fun**!" And about the reward kids feel in the partnerships with adults which develop through working together on a project or on a Round Square Committee. But a new item was: "are you going to talk about the **culture** of Round Square?" This is on the money; I must do so. And they made it clear they feel that the real "keepers" of the Round Square culture are each school's RS Reps.*
— Author's journal entry, October, 24, 2004

*Being at a Conference and meeting people from all over the world who all were from Round Square schools and really wanted to make a difference in the world was a very important experience for me. It made me realize how, if we commit ourselves, we really **can** make a large impact on today's society across the globe, and change things for the better.* — Female student, U.K.

§

The twenty-six group interviews conducted at seventeen schools during a five-month period were, as was the case with the questionnaires, aimed at finding specific answers to specific questions.

The sessions were designed to enable comparative assessment. For instance, each interview was framed and conducted in the same way, and addressed identical topics. There were variations, but all seemed acceptable. (For instance, some interview rooms were more suitable than others, some groups were more discursive or more task-oriented than others, and in quite a few cases, what seemed to be an irrepressible level of interest caused more participants to show up at a session than the dozen I had requested and the host school had selected.)

The four questions which I sought to address through these interviews were:

- What do students and graduates believe are the most important aims of Round Square?
- Based on their experiences, which aims do they believe that Round Square meets effectively, and where does its performance need to be improved?
- What words would students and graduates choose if asked to describe Round Square?
- What are the aspects of Round Square which are the most important for others to understand?

With these objectives in mind, a ninety-minute interview was designed. The interview design had four segments.

The first piece was an "ice-breaker." Students were invited to share with the group what they had written in Part II of the questionnaire. Doing so not only invited students to speak, but allowed me to gain entry to the group through focused attention (since I had these anecdotes on paper, I was able to listen without taking notes). The second segment began with the distribution of the "Seven Laws of Salem" which Hahn developed in the 1920's (see Chapter Two). This document was chosen because it expresses Round Square's purpose, but it is *not* a statement (such as the published "IDEALS") which students and graduates would recognize as a formal expression of Round Square as an organization.

I asked each participant to number Hahn's statements in order of what each felt should be the statement's priority for a Round Square school

(1 = most important, 7 = least important). When this had been done, each was asked to say what number he or she had assigned to the first statement. The numbers were recorded on a newsprint sheet as they were called. This process was repeated for each statement.

Next, I added up the numbers for each "Law." These sums were written on the newsprint sheet. The highest and lowest sums were identified and circled. These were proposed as the "group response," reflecting what the *group as a whole* felt about priorities which should be assigned to the various statements.

We then computed the *range of responses* (difference between highest number given by an individual participant, and the lowest) for each question.

Finally, I asked the group to identify the one or two goals expressed by the seven statements which, based on their own experience, are being most effectively met by Round Square, and one or two which "need more effort."

The third segment proposed that a book is to be written about Round Square. Being an academic book by an academic person, it "must" have a colon [:] in the middle of its title. The author has decided what comes *before* the colon; "Round Square." But he's stumped, and needs help. What suggestions would the participants offer for the rest of the title?

Of course, this felt like a game, and thus was fun. Usually there were at least as many suggestions as participants. (Some of these suggestions were *very* clever.) Finally, participants were asked to give me advice about the book which was about to be written. What should the book do? What should it *not* do? Advice always was forthcoming!

When the records of all twenty-six sessions were collected and analyzed, the findings were illuminating in a great many ways.

For example: the mean scores assigned by participants to each of the "Hahn laws" were strikingly similar. For all but two groups, the "most important" was the first (*"Give the students opportunities for self-discovery"*). On a scale in which "1" was the most important and "7" the least, the mean value assigned by 300 participants to this first statement was 1.9.

Three more "Laws" clustered between scores of 3.1 and 3.7 (in other words, they were given an above-average importance by participants). These were the second, third, and seventh "Laws:" *"Make the students meet with triumph and defeat;" "Give students opportunities for self-effacement in the common cause;"* and *"Free children of the wealthy and powerful from the enervating sense of privilege."*

When range of response (the span from lowest to highest score in any group) was examined, two findings popped out. The narrowest range was accorded to the first of the "Laws." The only other "Law" which had a mean range under 4 was the sixth: "Make games important but not predominant."

The widest range of response by nearly a whole point occurred on the last of the statements The range of response was, in fact, extraordinary. In nearly all groups, at least one participant felt this was the *most* important of the statements, and at least one felt it was the *least* important.

These findings suggest that:

• The overwhelming top priority given the first of the "Laws" by all groups tells us that **students and graduates believe that Round Square is for, and about, themselves.** For these young people, Round Square's most important outcome is the *self-discovery* which service, exchanges, adventure, or international connections produce.

This finding seems to align in a most interesting way with ongoing research about the way the human brain functions in relation to the development of the self. Scientists have long known that a pre-adolescent child's sense of himself or herself is far less developed than that of a teenager or adult, and that one of the main "tasks" of adolescence is establishing a more mature sort of identity. Researchers now know that the difference is based in brain development. They are able to see, using modern scanning technology, that an adolescent's brain becomes far busier than a child's brain does in the cellular areas which store and process information about the self. They have also found that, from adolescence onward, a person will not only respond in an intense and special way to situations which seem to relate to the self, but will also remember more from "self-related" experiences (including self-revelatory ones) than from other events. It follows that any activity which promotes "self-discovery" will seem highly important to a teenager, and that such experiences have a lasting power to drive learning.

Needless to say, students were speaking of Round Square as a source of self-discovery long before anyone began to look into the neurological basis of this phenomenon. But what the current research does help to explain is why the experiences which students and graduates tell us about so often have such importance for them, and why graduates report they continue to reflect on and learn from these experiences years later.

• For students and graduates, the statement regarding the appropriate role of "games" seemed to have little resonance. Discussions with graduates and students led me to suspect that the guidance they received before they responded — which was to consider all statements *in the light of their own experience* — may have "led" this response. What we might take this to mean is that, in Round Square schools, finding a proper role for sport has *not* been experienced by students as a problem. Sport *already has* a proper role.

• Finally, *students and graduates are of no single* mind about the importance of the proposed obligation to *"Free the children of the wealthy and powerful from the enervating burden of privilege."* A number of student participants clearly were reacting to the *wording* of the statement, expressing disdain for *any* proposal which could be seen as advocating a high priority for the needs of any one student sub-group, especially an advantaged one.

However, I also suspect that, despite the anti-elitist mindset documented by the questionnaire, there are unresolved concerns among these young people about how wealth, poverty, class, and privilege should be confronted and understood by students.

Each group was asked to decide which of the "Laws" is most successfully addressed by Round Square, and which needs more attention. *Every group without exception rated Round Square's performance in terms of student self-discovery as most successful*.

The next two most positively rated areas were the third of the statements, (*"Give students opportunities for self-effacement in the common cause"*) and the last *("Free the children..."* etc.). However, a number of groups chose to give *both* "plus" and "minus" ratings to the seventh of the "Laws." In fact, this "Law" not only tied for second-highest in "plus" ratings (*effective performance*), but it led in "minus" ratings (*should do better*). In other words, students and graduates agreed that this objective, about which they had differed widely as individuals, was *both* something Round Square does commendably, *and* something it needs to do better.

The "complete the title" exercise was fun, but also fascinating.

Students and graduates showed that they conceive of Round Square in ways which are consistent with views expressed in the previous segment of this interview. Round Square most fundamentally involves one's own experience; it produces self-discovery; it connects one to the world and to life; it is a kind of learning where volition matters; and it can reward the person who will take a plunge into adventure.

Of the words / phrases most often used by participants in the titles which were proposed to follow the words "Round Square," the most frequent were the following (with numbers of times each was mentioned): *Experience (15); World (11); Life, living (11); Student (10); Self-discovery (9); Learning (9); Opportunity (8); Discovery (7).*

As one might expect in groups which included so many smart, imaginative young people, there were some intriguing (and revealing) suggestions. Some of my favorites were:

> *Expanding Your Own Frontiers*
> *A Global Community*
> *Ideals, Impressions, Realizations*
> *There's One World!*
> *Life Changing*
> *Doing Something for the Greater Good — if You Dare*
> *Thinking Globally — and Acting on It*
> *Imagine…***More***!*

The last segment of the interview design asked for advice. Here the purpose was to identify what students and graduates feel most needs to be more widely understood about Round Square. Once again, words and concepts, when seen all together, suggest what students and graduates think Round Square really *is*. Here are some examples:

> *Don't imply that you have to go around the world to be part of Round Square*
> *Include pictures (of kids doing things!)*
> *Be concrete (not theoretical)*
> *Relate IDEALS to actual events*
> *Use examples — tell stories*
> *Make sure it's clear that Round Square offers "a space to grow into"*
> *Focus on individuals*
> *Don't omit problems or weaknesses*
> *Make the students the main point*
> *Say how it all came to be — origins and ideals really matter*
> *Use simple language as much as possible*
> *Be sure to say that Round Square is **fun**!*

§

The group interviews also offered a chance to compare the views of students and graduates. While the questionnaires suggested that there would be a high level of similarity, the statistics which led to that conclusion depended on a smaller-than-ideal number of graduates, so a test of this finding was important.

The responses of graduates to the various phases of the group interview did indeed show a high level of similarity. This added credibility to the earlier indication that the views of students at Round Square schools persist after they graduate. For example, the pattern of question-by-question responses of graduates in ranking the significance of the seven "Laws" mirrored the student pattern, and the mean response to each "Law" was close enough to student responses to make numerical differences insignificant. The same pattern held true for range of response item by item, and for response range as a whole.

There was, however, one interesting difference. This related to the last of the Hahn "Laws." While graduates' rankings resembled the students' responses, their mean assessment of the importance of the seventh of the "Laws"— *"Free the children of the wealthy and powerful from the enervating burden of privilege"* — placed a substantially lower value on it than the assessment made by students (4.9 points on a 1 = high, 7 = low scale, compared to 3.7 for students). Do graduates see the effects of socio-economic and class differences as being inherently less important than students do? Or are they telling us that they see what schools can teach us in a different manner?

One way to examine this issue is to separate all of the "Laws" which were given a higher value by graduates than by students from those which were assigned a lower value by graduates than by students, even if the rank-order is the same, and consider what these numerical differences, however small, might suggest.

Graduates assigned a higher value to the first two of the "Laws" (*"Give the students opportunities for self-discovery,"* and *"Make the students meet with triumph and defeat"*) and to the fifth (*"Train the imagination"*). All are very much concerned with the school's promotion of an *individual student's* self-discovery and personal development. On the other hand, graduates gave lower ratings to three other items (*"Give students opportunities for self-effacement in the common cause,"* *"Make games important but not predominant,"* and *"Free children of the wealthy and powerful from the enervating burden of privilege"*). All of these "Laws" are less concerned with the individual development of the student than with his or her socialization.

These graduates seem to be telling us that they look back on their secondary schooling in a way which is not quite the same as how current students see it. Why? The answer is grounded in human development. A normal teenager tends to see what he or she is doing in terms of exploring a whole world, without and within, and establishing reality in both. The young adult is more apt to look back on what was learned in adolescence as leading not so much to reliable knowledge of the world (discoveries made in adolescence have usually been modified by subsequent experience) as to self-discovery.

On the whole, what is really remarkable about this population of students and graduates is the persistence of values and attitudes over time. The research demonstrates that Round Square's effect on the basic views of students who are involved in its world of "IDEALS" is not only intense at the moment, but will have a consequence which will be durable.

It's not just students who were apt to use the term "life changing" to describe the impact of a Round Square experience. Graduates did so, too.

§

Much of this chapter has had to do with means, averages, and statistics. All have great power to reveal patterns and make sense of complex phenomena. But in thinking this way, we can obscure valid differences and particularities. Round Square is a *movement*. It is not a system, or an organization which resembles a franchise-based corporation. Its schools are heterogeneous.

For this reason, the actual world of Round Square's schools can never be fully understood in terms of means and averages. There are not only overt and important differences — contrasts of national and regional settings, sizes and styles, day and boarding schools, boys' schools, girls' schools, and coed schools, etc. — but there are also grand and famous schools as well as younger and less well-known ones. Round Square includes schools with religious affiliations as well as non-sectarian schools — urban, suburban, rural and outback schools — First World and third world schools — and so on. And beyond all that, there are subtle but no less meaningful differences, including between those which seem to be deeply driven and holistically shaped by their Round Square involvement, and those which seem less completely explained by the Round Square relationship.

No attempt was made to "measure" these school-to-school contrasts. However, such differences could not escape notice as I traveled from campus to campus and listened to conversations with students and graduates. Over time, impressions naturally formed. During one long, transcontinental plane ride, I set these down in my journal:

> *There is a considerable variability in the degree to which Round Square penetrates the total fabric and ethos of any one school. Many of the adults I have listened to say this is school-size related. My own reading is that it isn't, really. Rather, my conversations with students in particular suggest that it has more to do with four other factors: (1) the makeup, structure, personal qualities and actual responsibilities of the student Round Square committee at each school, and how this committee connects with the Round Square Rep and the Head; (2) the stature and capabilities of each Rep, and how he or she interfaces with those who lead Round Square activities, and all other programs within the school; (3) the extent to which a school uses its internal / external messaging to feature, explain, and promote Round Square involvement and achievement; and (4) attitudes toward Round Square which are expressed by the Head and the Governors.*
>
> *I've seen schools both large and small which are extraordinarily effective in each of these ways, and it's paying off — Round Square is a **mine** of value for them. Other schools (of various sizes) seem less fully or evenly engaged, but most appear to be conscious of deficits and are in hot pursuit of those they see as important.*
>
> *There's also an apparent difference in the personal impact on individual lives that's described by the kids who have been on major service projects (whether a project has been sponsored by RSIS, regions, or individual schools seems irrelevant) and those students who have **not** had a serious service "adventure," even if they have exchanged, gone to a regional or international Conference, been on an expedition, etc. While all students are apt to eagerly claim great benefit from what they've done, those who've been involved with service have often been stirred **deeply** — they seem to have been caused to re-think and revise some of their most basic ideas (such as those concerning class / culture / socioeconomic matters) to a degree that's less apparent in others. So, I suspect that the number which really drives Round Square's impact on a school isn't size at all, but (after one accepts the importance of the four variables listed above) its ratio of*

students participating in major service projects compared to total school population. — Author's journal, November 11, 2004

Months later, during another long plane trip, I looked back at the same pages, and added the following:

*First and foremost, Round Square is consistently explained by students as being **about them**. It's about their own self-discovery and their adventure of growing up and into the world. **This is the universal, main message.***

Round Square is advantaging every one of the schools I visited, but is doing so in different ways. It's not as simple as "a lot" or "a little." These differences also have less to do with nationality or first-world / third-world contrasts than I had expected, and more to do with stages of institutional development at each school.

*Round Square is not a "one size fits all" organization. Neither is it suited to only one "kind" of school. A fundamental reason for its "adaptability of benefit" seems to be Round Square's sustained focus on **goals** as contrasted to **methods**. For an organization in a professional sector — K-12 Education — that has a long history of a relentless lust for the orthodox, Round Square has been astonishingly able to accept differences.*

Even so, the students are right: there are not only clear, shared aims linking these schools, but a shared culture too. That raises my concern in relation to the march of globalization, which is without question a powerful force accelerating Round Square's growth. Right now, being able to present a school as "global" has marketing juice. However, this may before long attract schools to Round Square which want this cachet, but in fact are less than vigorously focused on Round Square's goals, nor may they really be focused on their students and the personal development of these individual young people which can be promoted through their being "impelled into experience." I saw no opportunist schools in these visits; but Round Square will have to be prudent and cautious in this regard if its profoundly important "soul" of integrity of purpose is to be preserved…

*Finally, looking back through all these pages, the **critical importance of service as a fundamental factor in this*** *movement's identity* keeps announcing itself. That's not just a matter of history. It's what kids say — right now.

International service is clearly the most powerfully transformative experience which happens to individual youngsters among all of Round Square's programmatic components. A service experience which takes a young person out of the familiar world of school, nation, culture, and socio-economic situation, and places him or her for a significant time in an unfamiliar part of the world, doing hard work and living simply in the "area beyond the comfort zone" with a highly diverse group of peers, has been and continues to be the beating heart of Round Square.

It seems evident that Round Square will have to place a high priority on being tolerant of innovation and willing to take risks, and be visionary, too, in devising strategies to support expansion of its service undertakings in the next decade or so. It will need to assure that as pressures to expand are met, this core part of what it does for students is well and prudently managed, and is able to have a real impact, year after year, student after student, for enough students at every member school to continue to define and energize what the young people themselves believe "Round Square" means — because, in the end, **the students' definition is the only one that matters.**
— Author's journal, April 4, 2005

We'll let the last words in this chapter on the student / graduate perspective be these:

*Being at the '04 Conference was **amazing**! I had never realized how big Round Square is, or how large its impact is. Having so many people from all around the world in one place, learning and making friends, was so cool! From the Conference I learned that sometimes in life we are trapped inside our own little bubbles, unaware of what's going on around us. We **must** find the strength to break out, as there's a world outside, just waiting to be discovered!* — Female student, U.K.

Chapter Seven:
A Final Three Schools —
Schüle Schloss Salem, Deerfield Academy, Gordonstoun School

I T'S THE END OF A SPRING FRIDAY MORNING AT SCHÜLE SCHLOSS SALEM, a school nestled among low hills, tidy vineyards, orchards, and newly-plowed fields in Baden, a few kilometers from the Bodensee in the southwestern corner of Germany. Students in their middle teens are streaming away from classes. They're not just on the brink of a weekend, but it's a lovely, sunny day — so they converge enthusiastically, chatting and calling to each other, as they cross a vast courtyard toward the *essaal*, or campus dining room, where they'll have a loud, joyful lunch together.

Excited, happy kids: springtime. It's a universal scene. No matter which continent we're on, the sound of youthful high spirits at such a time of day, week, and year is always the same. However, if a visitor knows the history of this particular place, that notion is also oddly jarring.

Schüle Schloss Salem's immense complex of masonry buildings was originally built centuries ago not as a school for noisy teenagers, but as a workplace and spiritual retreat for a community of monks who spent their lives here, at what was one of Europe's great Cistercian abbeys. And despite 85 years of tenancy, the school has done little to change one's first impression. The place still *looks* monastic. The huge ring of inward-facing abbey buildings, all decorated in a harmonious baroque fashion, seems more likely to house a religious community than a group of giddy youngsters. A gray gothic church at the middle of the courtyard presents a stark visual contrast to the baroque grace of the rest of the complex — just as it was certainly meant to do, centuries ago. And when one follows Salem's students into a sprawling building which was once the administrative center of the abbey, and now serves the same function for the school, one sees that many of the classrooms and offices open on halls and cloisters which are still decorated with paintings and frescoes left behind by the monks. Today's students even live behind the massive doors which once opened to the monks' sleeping quarters.

Past and present don't conflict at Salem. They commingle.

Of course, the monks are long gone from Schloss Salem, but the Markgraf of Baden, whose family took the abbey over when the Cistercians departed, and whose grandfather founded Schüle Schloss Salem with Kurt Hahn shortly after World War I, is still the school's landlord. Salem is intensely conscious of all aspects of its heritage, and especially of Hahn's legacy. A room in the library at its Spetzgart campus is devoted to an expansive Hahn archive (within which there is a large and useful section about Round Square). The current Markgraf isn't just the estate's owner, either; he lives at Schloss Salem, and operates its farming enterprises, including a wine-making business, in some of the other old buildings facing the courtyard. These structures, built as barns by the monks hundreds of years ago, continue to serve agricultural purposes today.

So this, the original Salem campus, not only ties this school to a distant past, but to its early days as an institution, and to a complex present. School and abbey, school and farm / winery, school and aristocratic landlord in a post-aristocratic democracy: all are in one place, together.

Salem has another tie to history which most German visitors will know about. Created in the 1920's by Kurt Hahn, as headmaster, and the Markgraf of Baden, as board chair, Salem was meant to provide a different kind of education than that which was offered at other top-level German schools. This school proposed something radically new — not just to pursue academic excellence, but to be *equally* concerned with nurturing strength of character, a sense of social responsibility, personal independence, and the ability to act according to one's conscience (instead of through dutiful obedience, which had been a national norm).

With such objectives, it surprised no one that Salem and its headmaster (who was seen as unacceptable not just because he was advocating "un-German" ideas, but because he was Jewish) were early and obvious targets for the wrath of the Nazi party. Before long, Hahn had been jailed, and then was forced to flee to Britain. The Nazi government soon launched a campaign to redefine and re-shape this renowned but "unacceptable" school. Amazingly, when World War II ended, and the school's Nazi staff had departed, it became clear that the spirit of Schüle Schloss Salem, though forced underground during the war years, had survived. Soon a cadre of old Salem staff and new leaders and teachers (some of whom were Salem graduates) arrived to rebuild and restore the school. Before long, Salem was back in the first rank of German schools, again able to present a vivid and unusual example of innovative, deeply purposeful education, which is as concerned with maximizing human development and educating for democracy as it is with academic achievement.

Just as Salem's students present a marked contrast to the tenants of the old abbey, the Salem of the twenty-first century, even if it fully retains its purpose and spirit, is beginning to develop contrasts with its own past.

Schüle Schloss Salem, which continues to be a boarding school, now has *four* campuses — the original one at the abbey, or Schloss Salem, which is home to students in the early part of secondary school; Hohenfels, an ancient castle on a crag above the Danube valley, perhaps a dozen kilometers away, which houses the lower grades; Spetzgart, about the same distance away, but overlooking the Bodensee, near Uberlingen, which is the home of Salem College, the upper-grades part of the school; and Haerlen, a ten-minute walk toward Uberlingen from Spetzgart, which houses grade 13 students (the classrooms and facilities of Spetzgart and Haerlen are used by all students who reside on the two campuses).

Hohenfels Castle is a story-book location for younger students. One can easily imagine a German Harry Potter peering from its arrow-ports. Spetzgart, the older part of which was built to be a resort hotel, has a more grown-up and sophisticated feeling — and a more suburban tone than the rural / monastic Schloss Salem campus or the knights-in-armor fantasy-land of Hohenfels. In contrast to them all is Haerlen, a spanking new, low-slung, minimalist-modern cluster of white buildings which could easily be mistaken for a corporate headquarters or a high-tech factory. Located at the edge of Uberlingen, the Haerlen campus feels urban and adult. It proclaims itself as a workplace, rather than as a medieval playhouse, rural retreat, or lakeside resort.

It's been said that "architecture is destiny" for schools. If so, then Salem's four distinct campus segments are shaping a very unusual destiny for this great boarding school. The Salem of today seems content — even eager — to leave behind conventional assumptions about education, and particularly those which imply that a good school must seek institutional unity by presenting a consistent culture and constant expectations to all its students. Admittedly, Salem's four-campus configuration was not formed according to a single plan or purpose. Some of Salem's various bits and pieces were acquired to meet other needs than those they now serve, and the Haerlen campus was built so the school would be able to relocate if a protracted conflict between Salem's Board and the current Markgraf had not been settled amicably. But — original intentions notwithstanding — Schüle Schloss Salem has by now arrived at a physical arrangement which uniquely expresses a "developmental" progression in the settings and educational cultures its students will encounter. Young people move from campus to campus during their time at Salem, just as they move from one stage of growing-up to another. They start in the castle of childhood at Hohenfels, and end up in the quasi-corporate environment of Haerlen.

In his office on the Schloss Salem campus, Bernhard Bueb, who when we spoke was about to retire as Headmaster of Salem after more than two decades in that role, characterized Salem's multi-campus expansion and the resulting developmental stratification of the school as "a dynamic process." "You can't hinder an organization which is being driven from within to expand in this way," he said, even though the changes are forcing the school to keep "looking for new forms of doing things."

Thinking back over Salem's long history of affiliation with Round Square (it was one of the founding schools), Bueb firmly characterized Salem as "greatly benefiting" from its connection to a community of peer schools around the world. He especially cited Round Square's support for international exchanges ("*very* important for us — and it's clear that many of the other Round Square schools feel the same way"), international service ("of great value to our staff as well as to students"), and the increasingly rich experience of the international Conferences each year ("the Conferences have become better and better."). He also felt the expectation that each school's students raise money every year to support service projects is "a good thing for them" as it helps to sustain and broaden interest and excitement about Round Square in the school — "we've had trouble at times in the past sustaining involvement between Conferences." Round Square, in his view, is by now wholly "integrated" as a core part of life at Salem, and is especially valuable because it is something that connects the larger world to *all* Salem students. The school's other notable international connection (to the International Baccalaureate program) directly affects only those who are enrolled in the IB curriculum.

Dieter Plate, Head of the Spetzgart / Haerlen ("Salem College") part of the school, and another long-time Salem leader who was about to retire, agreed with Bueb's assessment. When I asked him to identify problems, past or present, in making Round Square work effectively for Salem, Plate quickly referred back to a time when Round Square was a smaller and more European group of schools, within which "the English schools dominated." During that period it was hard for Salem to see itself as "an equal part of the Round Square community," he said. "But now Round Square is really global." He feels the change has benefited both Salem and the organization. "I've been a friend of Round Square from the beginning," he said, but added that the rewards of this friendship for Salem are "much easier" to demonstrate to parents and students now than had been the case two decades ago.

Three RS Reps connected Salem with Round Square at the time of my visit. Maggie Chodak and Ulrike Niederhofer were based at the Schloss

Salem campus, and Helen White was at Spetzgart. Though they focused on different age groups; they were of one mind about Round Square's importance for Salem. Here are some key observations:

- Round Square's expansion is a benefit to Salem ("it's *good* to grow") but makes the work of RS Reps more challenging, as they must scramble to connect with new colleagues and "anticipate" new ideas and opportunities.
- More international service opportunities are needed ("lots more kids from Salem and probably from all the schools could, and *should*, go on projects").
- "Adventure is Salem's weak area in the IDEALS framework."
- Regional Conferences for younger students, which have been so successful in several areas, need more attention in Europe. "Our younger students are becoming much more involved and interested in Round Square...so there's an opportunity, and a need to be addressed."

Another Salem staff member, Karl Roth, has been deeply involved in Round Square as the adult leader of the multi-year nature-reserve rehabilitation effort at Boronka, Hungary. Roth, a veteran Salem science teacher, clearly is a gifted and inspiring educator, and he is profoundly invested in the Boronka service program. During my meeting with Roth, I never did manage to lure him into making a grand assessment of Round Square or toward discussing Round Square's over-all effect on Salem. Instead, he kept leading us both back to Boronka: to maps of Boronka, slides of kids working at Boronka, stories of improving links to local and Hungarian organizations, objectives for the upcoming year's project, and beautiful photos of the birds and wild animals whose lives depend on Boronka's preservation. We were just starting on a file of media clippings about the Boronka project when our scheduled time ran out.

In the end, the reflections about Round Square and service project leadership which I'd sought from Roth were never attained. But on the other hand, I came away full of respect for Roth and the Boronka project, and aware that if anyone wants to understand the special and inspired kind of adult leadership which is needed to sustain first-rate service learning, he or she needs only travel to southwest Germany, look up Karl Roth, and listen.

Conversations with student groups at both the Schloss Salem and Haerlen campuses were interesting, and not just because nearly all such discussions with young people at every Round Square school proved to be so, but because of the particular "take" on Round Square which many of the Salem students expressed. Within most student groups I interviewed at other schools, the most dramatic and powerful stories about growth and adventure tended to come from those students who had been on international service projects in countries such as India, or Kenya, or Thailand. But much of the energy in the discussions at Salem came from students who'd *exchanged* to other Round Square schools.

One of the students described an exchange experience to South Africa as "very difficult...but in a *good* way." Another, who had gone to Australia, talked about how it was "scary at first...but after a while, I realized I was welcome." A third, who'd gone to India, reported about how "illusions were broken. I realized how *German* I am."

These statements reminded me, again, of how a single program can create value for students at different schools in different countries in markedly dissimilar ways. Salem students are a gifted bunch of youngsters, academically and in many other ways. In their own school setting they radiate an almost glossy confidence. But many seem to have been startled and deeply challenged in ways they hadn't expected when they embarked on an exchange term at schools in another part of the world. The personal result, in every case, was described by students as one that led to "learning" and "growing." And as I listened, I began to better understand why Salem's Headmaster had started his recitation of the "benefits of Round Square" with enthusiasm about student exchanges. Exchanges appear to meet a particularly important need for Salemers, as perhaps they would for all young Germans; and these exchanges certainly have provided powerful learning experiences for a great many of them.

Later, I had an extended conversation with a Salem graduate who, in 1972, had traveled to the Athenian School in America to take part in a Round Square Conference. This was the first Conference where each participating school was asked to send students not as "observers," but as full *delegates*. Walter Sittler, who is now a well-known actor in Germany, related how, as Salem's student delegate in his final year, he had traveled across the Atlantic and the United States to represent Salem at Athenian's California campus. He recalled it as "a time when students at Salem [wanted to] participate much more." What he saw at Athenian was "a great shock — and a *very* hopeful one." There was what he felt was "an almost naive openness between those present, including openness between kids and adults" which seemed "wonderful."

But, he recalled, it was very hard to explain what he had experienced to other students and staff when he arrived back in Germany. "They too were looking for this very kind of change — *but*."

Now, thinking back more than thirty years to the Conference experience, he suspects that a large part of what he had seen at Athenian was a climate created by adults and students who believed it was professionally acceptable to "act as if they *liked* each other, and that the adults openly *loved* the subjects they taught. "But I was not only young then; I was alone when I tried to explain these things" back in Germany, he added. "I think that sending groups of students to Conferences, as schools do now, is a great improvement."

The 1972 Round Square Conference was one of the most powerful parts of his Salem education, Sittler says, and one he still thinks about. "It's in many of my memory files," he said. "And those files have helped me again and again to search for what I'll be doing next."

What does Round Square mean to today's Salem students? Suggestions made during two group interviews, one at Schloss Salem and one at Haerlen, seemed to answer that question: *Preparation for Life; Opportunity to Discover; Ideals, Impressions, Realizations; Meaning — for Past, Present, and Future; The Actual Thing.*

§

Another season, another school. Outside my window, it's a bright, cold winter morning at Deerfield Academy, in rural Massachusetts. The late-arriving sun is just peeking over a range of hills which hem in the valley. Below my window, boys and girls in brightly-colored winter jackets walk briskly — some run as eight a.m. nears — toward their first classes of the day. Through my room's frosted panes they appear to be moving dots of brilliant color against the stark white of new snow, framed by the inky lines of tall bare trees and a clear blue sky.

About them is their school — and seamlessly blending with it, the buildings of Old Deerfield. This village is (for the United States) an ancient place. Deerfield was once an embattled seventeenth-century frontier outpost of the Massachusetts colony, and a century later, a crossroads farming village in one of New England's most fertile valleys. Scores of old homes, many of them over three centuries old, line the village's mile-long main street. Built to be the residences of prosperous farmers who once inhabited Deerfield, some are now foundation-maintained museums, while others house Academy employees or remain as private homes. All are painstakingly restored, and lovingly kept.

The over-all effect is harmonious and peaceful, non-contemporary, and perhaps even other-worldly. For instance, although throngs of commuters are at this moment driving to work in nearby towns, their cars don't pass on the quiet street below me, although for centuries the region's main north-south traffic was routed along it. And then, there are no overhead electric or phone wires, or modern-looking streetlamps. Decades ago, to preserve the "historic" appearance of Old Deerfield, the main highway was moved to the eastern edge of the village, all wires were buried, and "modern" utility equipment was replaced by older looking fixtures. And although many of the dormitory buildings are actually modern masonry structures, they don't *look* new — or even much like school buildings. That's because they were cloaked in colonial-style wood or brick veneers when they were built, to resemble and "blend in with" Old Deerfield's genuinely antique structures.

The Academy itself is a venerable institution. During the eighteenth century, when government-run secondary schools had yet to be developed in America, the polymath writer, inventor, politician, and publisher Benjamin Franklin began to advocate for "town academies" as a way to broaden access to secondary schooling and, for some youngsters at least, the opportunity to prepare for university study. These "academies" would be independently governed, philanthropically-based free schools, open to any qualified student from the immediate area, with tuition fees to be paid by local taxpayers. Only sixteen years after the United States won independence, Deerfield was established as a "town academy."

For much of the next century, Deerfield Academy was seen throughout New England as a fine school. But then, as the agricultural economy in New England faded and government-run secondary schools began to take root, the academies — "private schools with a public purpose" — started to be seen as outmoded institutions. Consequently, when in 1902 a brand-new graduate of nearby Amherst College arrived to be Headmaster (and in a move aimed at economy, Librarian!) of Deerfield Academy, the school was beset by declining enrollment, inadequate financial resources, a worn-out plant, and collapsing community support. Its plight wasn't unique. A growing number of the state's political leaders were beginning an effort to force the Boards governing the town academies either to turn these institutions over to the government so they could become conventional government high schools, or abandon taxpayer support, which would make them fully private schools supported by tuition fees. The third alternative, of course, was simply to shut the academies' doors.

In 1902, the last alternative appeared the most likely destiny for

Deerfield Academy. However, against all odds, the diminutive and unprepossessing new Headmaster, Frank Boyden, not only preserved the Academy, and managed to keep it alive as a privately funded school when the Massachusetts government finally outlawed public funding of town academies; he went on during the next sixty-six years to develop Deerfield Academy into a unique and wholly excellent "national" boarding school.

Boyden did so by using an approach to the youngsters who came to Deerfield (and who were, in his early years there, likely to be cast-offs from the country's "top" schools) which was at once pragmatic, intellectually and physically demanding, highly active, just as highly structured, and attentive to the welfare of each individual. His explicit object was developing good character in each and every student. This meant the inculcation through day to day experience at Deerfield of what Boyden saw as the values which had helped build democracy in America, and which would be needed to sustain it. These were the "attitudes toward life" which would persist long after schooling had ended — integrity, firmness of purpose, courage, respect and concern for others, and a kind of flexible community-mindedness which Boyden often encouraged through such Delphic maxims as "be mobile."

The students Boyden wanted in his school were those in whom he saw "promise," which might be summed up as a mixture of intelligence, physical robustness, and grit, along with some evidence of an ability to respond to his school's particular approach. Boyden was inclined to accept promising applicants without regard to their families' ability to pay. Thus, Deerfield enrolled not just children of the social and economic elites, who in the early twentieth century populated most other American boarding schools, but a community of students selected on the basis of what he believed to be their evident *potential*.

The pursuit of such a relatively egalitarian vision required masses of money. Money was needed to build a capable plant where there was none, and to fund annually an operation which, due to Boyden's commitment to socio-economic inclusion and thus to financial aid, was expensive to run. To meet this need, Boyden (and later, Deerfield as an institution) became one of the great examples of successful American fund-raising. Today Deerfield remains an organization of legendary prowess in this area (at the time of my visit, a brand new, state-of-the-art science center, was being built). But the school is still known for admitting applicants without regard to their families' ability to pay.

Boyden, in collaboration with those who were working to preserve Old Deerfield as a historic site, was also able to encourage those with little or no philanthropic interest in education to fund a village ambience for his school by restoring Deerfield's trove of old buildings. As a result the school became, and remains, unique: part rural retreat, part live-in museum, part top-level academic center, part personal-development hothouse. Uniting all these characteristics, the school's motto is "Be Worthy of your Heritage."

So what I saw outside my window on a winter morning in 2005 was not just a lovingly preserved old New England village, nor a highly selective, splendidly equipped, diversely populated twenty-first century national school, but a fusion of those elements. The combination has led Deerfield to be one of America's most distinctive, sought-after, and respected boarding schools.

Yet, with eminence comes peril.

As the twenty-first century approached, those who led the Academy were concerned that the school's abiding mission and concern for each individual student's character might require greater programmatic support, given Deerfield's highly competitive admissions and its reputation for top-tier university placements. At the same time, Head of School Eric Widmer (Deerfield Class of 1957) was concerned that Deerfield students would need a more profound connection with and comprehension of the world beyond the school's small New England village. Widmer and his Board were especially concerned that Deerfield's students be fully prepared to live in, respectfully understand, effectively serve, and provide leadership in the "globalized" world society which the new century was producing. That led Deerfield to investigate Round Square in the 1990's. The school gained membership in 2001.

Widmer, a large, stooping, soft-spoken man who navigates his campus, even in the snow, on a bicycle (Boyden, just as idiosyncratically, used a horse and buggy), now sees the consequence of Deerfield's decision to join Round Square, which was a rare step for a school which has not been a "joiner," as all he'd hoped for, and more. He's watched Deerfield students eagerly participating in exchanges and projects. They have attended and been active participants in six Conferences. And the experience of hosting an annual Round Square Conference at Deerfield in 2004 was, in his view, an especially powerful learning experience for the entire school community. It not only welded 40 students and several staff members into a leadership team which worked collaboratively on planning and running the Conference; this same group also created a new understanding within the school of what an ambitious adult / student "partnership" could accomplish. The model presented by the way the Conference was developed and managed, Widmer realized, had substantially advanced his school's ability to train students for life, service and leadership in a democracy and a global society.

Deerfield's RS Rep is its Associate Head of School, Martha Lyman. While sharing Widmer's enthusiastic appraisal of the value produced during the school's early years of involvement in Round Square, she also sees the evolution of Round Square at Deerfield as "a work in progress." For instance, it continues to be difficult for Deerfield to coordinate the various administrative operations which provide student accommodations in order to set aside as much housing for incoming exchange students as Lyman would consider appropriate. There are "timing problems" involving coordination with academic and extracurricular programs which inhibit departures of some students who have wanted to go on exchanges and service projects. And she frequently encounters "parental resistance" when children announce they want to exchange or spend a month on a service project in a distant part of the world.

Part of this latter problem, Lyman said, "is just perfectly understandable anxiety — the kids want to go off into what we *all* know is a dangerous world." But the resistance is also based on the reluctance ambitious parents of talented children feel when they are asked to relax an approach to parenting that has rewarded them for stressing, or perhaps overstressing, messages to their offspring such as "focus on priorities" and "stay on track." Lyman believes that Deerfield's parents need "clear and understandable information" about what the real, long-term value of Round Square experiences will be. No such resource now exists — and Deerfield is still too young in its affiliation with Round Square to have built up the deep-seated community of informed parents which, at many other Round Square schools, can help worried moms and dads "get the picture."

She agreed that having the Conference at the school "helped enormously" to advance understanding of and respect for Round Square among the teaching / coaching / dorm resident faculty. However, "not everyone is on board yet," she said. It's not always easy to accept that your best (or worst) student should miss a term of chemistry to study in Australia, or that service in Kenya should take priority over an athletic tournament. Yet, as seems to be the case with Deerfield's parents, what Lyman observes in the views of her colleagues suggests that the gradual aggregation of experience and understanding will, over time, answer this problem. In her words, Deerfield merely needs to "let it all seep in gradually" as the school moves past a sometimes puzzled or skeptical early acceptance of Round Square by students, parents, and teachers to a position of "real ownership."

Conversations with Deerfield students were, as Widmer predicted, greatly energized by the recent Conference experience. But what I heard from these young people was just as reflective and visionary as it was enthusiastic.

"The Conference made a really *huge* difference," one student said; "our *roots* deepened." There certainly was an electric sense of camaraderie and pride among those who'd been part of the Conference-organizing team. Yet, the same students also wanted to talk about their experiences in other Round Square activities, and to speculate about the deeper impact of these experiences. One spoke about a service project in South Africa: "a whole series of unexpected cultural shocks...a realization that community service is not just the practical task you perform, but an introduction to a whole new way of thinking about people and culture." A boy who'd been on a service project in Kenya to build a school for developmentally handicapped children found that the "culture shock" which most rocked him and his peers was the encounter it provoked with their own unexamined attitudes and biases about people with disabilities. And a girl who had been a Baraza-group discussion leader during the Conference talked about her discovery, through listening to her peers from other parts of the world, that there are strong, culturally-based differences in what had motivated individual youngsters to take part in a Round Square Conference, exchange, or project. Moreover, she had come during the Conference week to realize that each of the various motives she discerned might very well be entirely valid and legitimate. "We don't all necessarily have the same agenda." And because of this difference in personal "agendas," she speculated, "what you take away will always be somewhat personal and particular...because of the differences in *why* you came, and *what* you brought with you."

Instantly, another student chimed in that these differences, while real, are *not* ones which end up separating students into culturally defined segments, or excluding one student from another. "There is always *one thing* in common — that you are each testing yourself in an area beyond your own comfort level. And *that* is the shared experience that reminds you of your common humanity."

The students' suggestions for definitions in the "complete the title" exercise revealed Deerfield's energy as well as its intellectual substance: *Exploring our Frontiers; Journey to Self-discovery; Educating through Experience; Experiencing Other Worlds; Pillars of Integrity; Global Community.*

Each Conference host school tries, in a polite but nevertheless determined way, to "improve on the model" provided by past Conferences, so as to produce an experience which will be unique and memorable. One of the innovations Deerfield's planners made was to ask four young Academy graduates to return to tell those attending the Conference about what they had done in relation to the "IDEALS" *after* they had left school. It was instantly evident that the student delegates found this "message from the future" fascinating — and while students from every corner of the world sat on the edges of their seats to listen, the oldest of the four began talking about her work as the leader of a United Nations commission that is disarming tribal militias in Afghanistan. Two more young graduates spoke — one about work with AIDS sufferers in South Africa, and the other about his role in protecting forests in the state of Vermont. Then the youngest of the four, still a student at Yale, talked about a year she'd spent after graduating from Deerfield as a volunteer providing service to young mothers in Peru, and also about her continuing commitment to volunteer service in the U.S.A. Speaking directly to the student delegates, she said that the decisive moment in choosing to make these personal commitments was the experience she'd had at the 2001 Round Square Conference at St. Philip's College in Australia. "That Conference changed my life," she said.

Many heads nodded — including those of Deerfield delegates in the audience. The follow-up question — "will *this* Conference change *my* life?" — was from that instant in every youngster's mind. It was, as a veteran Head of school remarked, "a Round Square moment." Bringing about such "life changing" enlargement of an individual's sense of what is possible and personally *necessary* has been a fundamental ambition of Round Square ever since its beginnings. Causing just such an expansion of vision for each young person was the goal which led so many schools to send students to this Conference, and which also led Deerfield Academy, the oldest institution in the Round Square community, to become one of Round Square's youngest members.

As Deerfield is learning, Round Square is able to capture the imaginations of *adults* as well as students. A few months before my visit, Widmer — who was approaching what in the U.S. would be considered retirement age — announced that he and his wife Meera Viswanathan would leave Deerfield at the end of the 2005-06 academic year, so he could become the founding head of a new boarding school in Jordan. This school, meant to educate students from all parts of the Middle East, is to be named the King's Academy. King Abdullah of Jordan, Deerfield Class of 1980, has been the driving force behind the new school. King Abdullah recruited Widmer for this position, in part to access Deerfield Academy as a template for the ambitious and most unusual new institution which he is helping to create.

Widmer intends his Jordanian school to be an applicant for Round Square membership before long. And thus we can see how a new idea about students and schools, first imagined as a result of what happened to students during a service project on a Greek island in 1954, continues to spread, from person to person, school to school, and nation to nation.

§

It's late March on the edge of the Moray Firth, in northern Scotland. Winter is still departing from this high-latitude part of the world, but in the farmland which lies all about Gordonstoun School, tractors are chugging about, readying the fields for planting, wherever the earth has dried out sufficiently to support them.

On the campus, the Gordonstoun boys' field-hockey team is engaged in a playoff with another Scottish school which, if the match is won, will move Gordonstoun up the ladder toward a national championship. The game, fortunately, is played on the school's synthetic-turf pitch (it would otherwise be played in a sea of chilly mud). Around the playing field are scores of Gordonstoun students and adults, many of whom jump up and down — not just to show enthusiasm, although their enthusiasm is real, but also to keep warm. A raw northerly wind is blowing from the general direction of the frigid Moray Firth, just a moderate walk away.

Happily, Gordonstoun's side, though in some cases less athletically gifted than their opponents, play well and intelligently as a team, and emerge the winners of a close, intense game. Even more happily, the school's players and their fellow students conclude the event not with the chest-thumping antics and cruel jeers one all too often encounters in the wake of secondary-school athletic events, but with behaviors which show respect for their visitors and friendliness to a group of boys who have done well, even if they have lost.

Kurt Hahn, who founded Gordonstoun (and played on its first field-hockey team until Jocelin Winthrop Young, then the team's student captain, and later the Founder Director of Round Square, had the audacity to cut him from the squad), would have loved this well-played game, and also the Gordonstoun team's generous post-game behavior. "Make games important, but not predominant" was one of Hahn's maxims. So too was "Make the children meet with triumph and defeat." One senses that these objectives are at work in today's Gordonstoun. Sport has its proper place, but no more than that. And the students are obviously able to understand how both triumph and defeat *feel*. They have gained the poise and compassion one needs to hold firmly to a polite and kindly sort of sportsmanship, even at a giddy moment of victory such as this one.

That evening, when I sat down for a group interview with Gordonstoun students, the room was packed. Twelve students had been asked to attend. Seventeen showed up. It soon was evident that each of those present has something to say about a Round Square experience of her or his own, and each wanted enough to be heard and to be part of the dialogue to attend, invitations notwithstanding. Hahn would have liked this moment, too. We recall his command to "Give the children opportunities for self-discovery" and to "Train the imagination." Both self-discovery and the imagination had certainly been at work in forming the over-the-top attendance for the session!

The students' suggestions about possible "title conclusions" were interesting. Here are a few: *Education as an Adventure; Leading though Example; Two Steps Ahead in the World; What It's All About; Learning as an Experience; Fitting Round Pegs in Square Holes.*

One slim, rather shy student who recently participated in an RSIS service project in Thailand talked about how the "very physical" aspect of the work was at first "daunting...but the readiness of others to help and understand...made it possible for us all to feel we were in the same boat, and this led us to realize we could prevail." Another student spoke of what he experienced during a service project in South Africa. "We were laying bricks, to help some local people build a house," he said, when "as we were working together with the residents, we came to realize that the people who were really being helped weren't just the locals, but *us*." An exchange student from Canada told me about an outdoor adventure program which he'd been told was meant to help students work together and learn to "trust each other" — but, he says, "I found that the person who was hardest for me to trust was really *myself*."

As time ran out and the discussion ended, a student offered a final suggestion for this book. "Make the reader really *think* about the IDEALS!"

Gordonstoun itself is a stimulant to such thinking. For instance, one of Round Square's "IDEALS" is *Adventure*. This school's outdoor adventure program (where the ideas leading to the widely known Outward Bound movement were developed) is by now seventy years old, but it is still a bold, ambitious undertaking.

During my visit, I was able to look over one especially venerable component of Gordonstoun's adventure curriculum, the "seamanship program." This program begins with basic training for all students in groups of eight, using the school's "cutters" (actually large double-ended whaleboats, which can be rowed or sailed with a simple ketch rig). After that there will be at least one week-long cruise in the *Ocean Spirit of Moray*, a modern 80-foot, ocean-capable sailing vessel which can accommodate a crew of sixteen students, up to three mates, and a professional captain for extended voyages. (More time in both cutters and *Ocean Spirit* for longer journeys is possible, of course, and many interested students volunteer.)

I spoke at length about the seamanship program with Ian Lerner, Director of the school's sail training program, and skipper of *Ocean Spirit*. What was particularly striking about our conversation was the degree to which this professional seaman sees what he does at Gordonstoun (and what the adult leaders of the mountaineering and backpacking and kayaking programs do) *not* as providing an auxiliary or subsidiary element in an essentially academic institution, but as directing a primary source of learning which is "*integral with*" a Gordonstoun education. The adventure programs are not presented as extracurricular options. Rather, each provides an *essential piece* of a comprehensively focused, unified educational experience called "Gordonstoun."

Such program integration means, for example, that student absences from classes, sports, and other activities — which may extend to a week or more for sail training — are not causes for anxiety or sources of conflict ("they are really *built into* the overall schedule"). And the connection bears an unusual responsibility for adventure program leaders like Lerner. "The pay-off [of sail training, or any other adventure program] *must be generally positive* for each student, in the context of his or her whole education, and must be just as positive for the whole school."

I heard the same point of view when I spoke with students and adult leaders who were involved with one of the most established of Gordonstoun's community service programs, the Fire Service. This is a student-and-teacher-staffed, school-based volunteer fire department located on the Gordonstoun campus, whose mission is to protect the school and those who live there from fire and other catastrophes, and also to support other fire companies in the region as needed. The boys and girls who were suiting up for a training exercise when I visited were just as conscious of the "integral" value of what they were doing as Lerner had been when he spoke about seamanship. While they were all as cheerful and enthusiastic about this exciting duty as teenagers can be, it was clear that they took the responsibility which they held for the preservation of life and property very, very seriously.

A determination to delegate truly *vital* responsibilities to the young was a seminal part of the educational innovation Hahn wrought at both Salem and Gordonstoun. And the message visible in the faces of these young people on a March afternoon in Scotland was unmistakable. Like the students who lead their school and are called Guardians, the youngsters who staff the Fire Service are clearly aware that theirs is a responsibility not just to act and to lead, but to protect. Evidently, the innovation which had proved so powerful in the 1920's was still alive and well — and no less powerful as a stimulant for growth and learning in the twenty-first century than it had been three-quarters of a century earlier.

Each of the schools which have been profiled in these pages has had one or another characteristic strength which seems unique. Starehe's baraza-centred democracy might be one example. It is as singular as St. Philip's zealous embrace of the world beyond the isolation of Australia's "red center," or Athenian's steadfast pursuit of a detailed "40 year mission." The same could be said of Salem's "progress of life" itinerary for its students as they grow up through four distinct campuses and four increasingly mature ways of living. And in much the same way, the integrity of Gordonstoun's entire educational program seems the way in which this school is most striking.

Gordonstoun is determined to be viewed and experienced by its students in a unified, holistic way. Most schools have to struggle continually to express a culture which even half-earnestly supports all parts of a narrowly defined academic curriculum, much less a culture which presents *all* curricular, co-curricular and extra-curricular offerings as experiences of equal value which merit equal commitment from everyone involved. Gordonstoun actually *does* this.

The Gordonstoun administration's and the staff's respect for the integrity of each student's experience is everywhere evident. It shapes what adults do with their own responsibilities, and is expressed through the respect and support they accord each other. Students again and again reflect this collaborative ethos. Such a behavior by students should be no surprise — after all, the school's adults aren't just *professing* a common purpose and general responsibility; they are *modeling* it, day after day.

Mark Pyper, the school's Headmaster, sees Gordonstoun as having a similar duty to support and lead Round Square, and to do so in large part by proposing and modeling a collegial, supportive relationship in his school's interactions with the other Round Square institutions. Explaining this commitment to parents and students on a recent Opening Day, Pyper pledged to "continue to play a leading role in the Round Square movement, which now [is] a global partnership of international awareness and outlook." And, as was appropriate for the Headmaster of a school where the organization began and which was the source of Round Square's name, he added "it is rewarding to see our ideals being adopted in other parts of the world, and it gives us great strength and confidence."

Pyper himself has been a conspicuous actor in the efforts of the Round Square community and its governing Board during the last decade. He has chaired groups which developed a self-assessment process to support each school's involvement in and commitment to Round Square, and he led a strategic planning exercise aimed at preparing for the expansion, administration, and financing of a growing organization.

At the time of my visit, Scottish independent schools were facing considerable pressure to justify their status as "public charities." While, as is usually the case in matters of this kind, the central political issues seemed rather mutable, the most serious questions related to whether independent schools are truly providing a "public benefit" and the degree of accessibility they offer to children from low- and moderate-income families. Although Pyper by no means welcomed such a governmental distraction from his work with Gordonstoun's students, and would not suggest that his fellow educators have blind trust in the ability of Scottish politicians to develop wise responses to these policy questions, he sees Gordonstoun's historic commitments as having prepared it "to meet these challenges...because [doing so] would not involve a major shift in either philosophy or practice. We have always shared our resources and been keen to be a part of the local community." And, he went on, "Gordonstoun has always endeavoured — successfully — to provide a top class education to those who cannot afford it and an education in citizenship has always been at the heart of our ethos."

Gordonstoun's student body is in fact not just socio-economically inclusive, but remarkably international. One student summed up the result of this diversity and the integrative nature of her school this way:

> *I truly think that Gordonstoun is a microcosm of international politics. You see petty arguments and honest agreements between people from different cultures...I've learnt how important it is to really observe others and be aware of their ideas. Studying here has forced me to be patient and to learn the importance of compromise and mediation.*

From his office in a catacomb-like former pantry in the cellar of Gordonstoun

House, John Hamilton, a mathematics teacher and the school's RS Rep, has managed student exchanges and dispatched hundreds of students around the world to be volunteers. Although nearing retirement, he remains vigorously invested in Round Square work. He too feels a responsibility to care for and lead the growing Round Square community. He has helped to bind Gordonstoun to its colleague schools, and has been much valued as a mentor and supportive friend by other RS Reps. He has not only represented the worldwide RS Rep group on the Round Square Board of Governors, but he continues to lead an overseas service project in Asia each year. Hamilton is in all these ways one of the main players in a group of wise, long-sighted, deeply earnest men and women whose service as RS Reps in the member schools has done so much to make Round Square live, thrive, and impart powerful learning for young people all over the world.

It is, nevertheless, a tremendous amount of work. Why would this senior, securely employed, respected teacher add so much to his workload in this way, year after year? What's the reward? The following statement may help to explain the John Hamiltons of Round Square. It was made by a Gordonstoun student returning from service in Honduras. The project's work involved construction of a dormitory for students from impoverished homes at a school in Tegucigalpa:

> *Our work consisted mainly of brick-laying, making cement, and erecting scaffolding...we also took turns in domestic duties. As we looked at the dormitory in its almost finished state, we all felt a great sense of achievement — this dormitory would house eighteen boys from disadvantaged backgrounds. {On} our last night there, lots of photos were taken and many tears were shed as {we celebrated} friendships which had been forged between our group and our teenage Honduran hosts.*
>
> *The whole trip served to show us that possessions are meaningless and that what counts is the love we show for one another...I would like to think we have...played our own small part in this.*

That's the reward.

§

Salem, Deerfield, and Gordonstoun are eminent schools. Each occupies a position of distinction in its country, and is eagerly sought after by applicants. Each has facilities which are handsome and well kept. Each has an excellent staff, and graduates who are advantaged by the reputation of their school.

All these factors may prompt a question in some quarters similar to one asked of me by a seatmate on a long flight experienced while preparing this book. This man, a sophisticated, well-traveled businessman, had been quizzing me about why I was on a flight between Perth, Australia, and Johannesburg, South Africa. When he learned about this book, he asked which schools belong to Round Square. Not all were familiar to him, but when I mentioned the three profiled in this chapter, he recognized each.

At first his reaction merely suggested esteem. But before long, he asked the question which was on his mind. *"What's really in it for schools like these?"* He said he could see how Round Square would be a wonderful way to focus and improve a young school, and that it might help almost *any* school become more "well rounded" or "internationally attuned." But to his way of thinking, these three schools are already excellent. They are perceived as leaders. And, he guessed, Round Square must be a substantial expense for any school. *So*: he asked, how can Round Square really be *"cost-effective"* for Salem, Deerfield, or Gordonstoun?

I assured him that the administrators and governors of these schools have certainly asked the same question, and will continue to do so — and that they have more than enough wisdom and competence on hand to develop sound answers. But the question nevertheless remained in my mind. *How can one really pin down "what's in it" for any Round Square school?* How can those who lead and govern schools assess "cost effectiveness" in a way which might be concrete enough to satisfy the businesslike questioning of my companion?

So I asked each of the Headmasters of the three schools profiled in this chapter to address the *"what's in it"* topic. Each did. All responded in a markedly pragmatic manner, and in a way which reflected much prior thought about the question.

Their answers were uniformly positive — but *weren't* identical. All of the Headmasters did cite many of the same kinds of value as deriving from membership in Round Square, such as a reliable resource for arranging exchange and service opportunities, or a source of networking connections with comparable schools in different nations. But each proposed at least one particular, unique benefit that his school obtains. For instance, Round Square is seen as a much-needed internationalizing force at Salem. It is driving a sustained effort to improve "education for democracy" at Deerfield. And it is valued by Gordonstoun's leaders because the Round Square community "confirms" the school's aims and principles.

Nevertheless, there's more to the question, and it needs a full answer. *How can we fully assess "what's in it?"* Cost-effectiveness requires an understanding of cost. What might be a cost benchmark? While actual expenditures between differently structured schools in different nations are almost impossible to compare, due to the variety of currencies involved and a large number of basic operating differences, one yardstick suggested by Heads of Round Square schools is that the total annual cost of Round Square membership — for dues, school-paid expense for students' participation in programs, travel and other cash costs for staff involvement, and the cost allotted for the professional time of the RS Rep — turns out to be similar, in cash and manpower, to the cost of a "typical, major" interscholastic sport, or a high-profile arts program such as dramatics.

If that's an acceptable benchmark, then it would also be fair to say that the "cost-effectiveness" of Round Square in terms of outcomes for students should be *at least comparable* to the results of a "typical, major" sport or arts program.

I have already presented a good deal of information about the *outcomes* which Round Square can generate for young people. Are there comparable outcome data for major sports and arts in these schools? I've seldom seen anything of the kind. However, I heard no one at any school suggest that Round Square would trail *any* major sport or arts activity in such a comparison.

All schools have academic goals. The three schools which we have just profiled present high academic expectations. How does Round Square impact these?

Intuition would suggest that Round Square should be a "minus" factor — it absorbs time and resources which would otherwise go into instruction and study. However, there is a substantial body of research (in the U.S., see data collected through the NELS program) which suggests that a student's active involvement in extra-curricular programs at school predicts *higher*, rather than lower, over-all academic achievement. Using this yardstick, we can infer that involvement in Round Square (as well as in the "major" sports and arts) will probably *benefit*, rather than diminish, over-all academic attainment.

The usual explanation for this counter-intuitive finding is that the enthusiasm, confidence, and ambition promoted through challenging extra-curricular involvement promotes greater over-all ambition, and encourages an achievement-oriented self-perception.

However, recent research on the role of "a feeling of challenge" as a factor affecting achievement adds detail to this finding. A July 2005 study concerning high-school students in the United States, conducted by the National Governors' Association, surveyed more than 10,000 secondary-school students across the country. A large proportion of the students surveyed not only were disappointed in their secondary schooling, but almost two-thirds said they would *be more engaged and work harder if their schools were more challenging*. As an article in the *New York Times* reported, the key finding of this research was the discovery that *"young people want to be challenged more."*

What the study suggests is that a student's general motivation in school will be positively affected if she / he feels *personally challenged* by the experience of school. Any increase in the feeling of being challenged is likely to result in the betterment of a student's motivation and performance.

Such a finding will surprise no teacher at a Round Square school. All have learned to expect that, while the "distraction" caused by a student's involvement in an exchange, overseas service, or adventure, or as a result of Conference attendance, may pose short-term difficulty, these involvements predict a betterment of the student's final academic record.

Increasing a student's feeling of being personally challenged may not be hard to make happen at many secondary schools. (As the study suggested, in typical schools, even the presentation of somewhat more rigorous courses would probably result in higher ambition). But adding challenge for the relatively small number of bright students who are *already* strong scholars, and who are *already* achieving fine results in demanding schools, will be a more difficult task. For many of these students, raising the academic bar still higher via even more difficult courses may not be *felt* by them as a dramatic increase in *personal challenge*. It may even feel the opposite. But the energy residing within them *can* be tapped via involvement in the type of engaging, adventurous, and empowering experiences described in Round Square's "IDEALS." After all, a developmentally-driven need to explore the world, gain and use power, and connect to a larger society, is present within *all* adolescents, regardless of intellectual gifts. All young people need to feel challenged. Round Square is helping that need to be met for all students, in all its schools.

One veteran mathematics teacher spoke to me about the "synergy" he sees between a student's involvement in Round Square and the academic results the same student is likely to achieve in top-level classes. "Yes, schedulers have to build this aspect of each student's life into their designs, and yes, we [teachers] have to be flexible. But if each of us does our part, then this aspect of our school *really pays off for kids*."

Schools such as Salem, Deerfield, and Gordonstoun tend to be places which are sustained in excellence by a "momentum of achievement" — a morale through which strong performance motivates, rewards, and then promotes further increases in aspiration. At their best, such schools sweep students up in this morale, motivating and rewarding them as they advance toward ever-higher expectations. Over time, a student seems to internalize this process of challenges accepted and successfully met. That is what Frank Boyden of Deerfield was talking about when he spoke of the "attitudes toward life" which he wanted Deerfield to inculcate in every one of its students.

However, a "momentum of achievement" is not a perpetual motion machine. It needs a continual input of new energy. This energy flows from each new student's achievements and the shared excitement of living in a community that is in pursuit of high expectations.

In fact, all high-functioning human systems share this kind of "momentum." It is what organization theorist Jim Collins (author of *Good to Great*) calls "the flywheel effect." Collins likens this cycle of high-output morale to a giant flywheel. The leader of a merely "good" organization can nurture his group's growth toward being "great" by urging each person within the organization to take "steps forward" consistent with the organization's aims and strengths, then allowing the "visible results" of these steps to be seen by each. The result "energizes" all the organization's people, adding new power to the "flywheel" of shared high expectations. As Collins puts it:

> *When you let the flywheel do the talking, you don't need to fervently communicate your goals. People can just extrapolate from the momentum of the flywheel for themselves: "Hey, if we just keep doing this, look at where we can go!"*

This was no doubt the same kind of effect which Hahn had in mind when, speaking not just of students, or teachers, or Headmasters, or schools as institutions, but of them all — he said:

> *We are better than we know. If only we can be brought to realize this, we may never again be prepared to settle for anything less.*

That realization of the potential to be "better," in one student after another, is, in the end, the answer to "what's in it" for Round Square schools. They are using Round Square to promote something that's quite priceless for any high-achieving organization: an ongoing realization that, however *good* any one person or one school may be right now, they can all be *better than they know* tomorrow. And as Hahn predicted, once such a discovery is made, it's hard for those involved to settle for a "merely good" situation.

Chapter 8:
Being Challenged, and Needed

OCTOBER 2004. A dozen of us are grouped around a large, square table in a basement classroom. The moderator of this Baraza discussion is a blonde American girl who is obviously bright, encouragingly gentle, and at this moment, *very* patient. She's trying to encourage the students in the room to speak up. Among them are a boy from Canada, a quiet girl from Switzerland, a confident British boy, a shy girl from Japan, a smiling Peruvian boy, a jolly Australian girl who seems to need no encouragement at all, and an eager but rather tentative young fellow from South Africa.

It's hard work for our moderator. The students have just met each other. Nearly all are in the United States for the first time. Many are still trying to adjust to many hours of traveling from distant places. On the other hand, our moderator seems well-prepared. And while some in the group are more ready than others to speak, all have volunteered to be here. Beyond that, it's clear that each wants nothing more than to *connect* with this roomful of strangers.

The moderator knows that the five adults who are at the table (a Briton, a Canadian, an Indian, a South African and me) expect to join and support the discussion as peers, but will stay out of her way as the group's leader. That common intention is no coincidence. Round Square Executive Director Terry Guest has explicitly reminded all of us that our purpose in being at this table is to *join*, rather than *take over*, what is meant to be a student-driven experience.

Minutes pass, slowly at first. We introduce ourselves. With the leader's support, the bolder ones speak up, and a few hesitant interpersonal connections are made *("Hey — I knew the girl who was on exchange from your school to mine last term...she was super")*. And before long the ice, which was never very thick anyway, has thawed. We are on our way to becoming a little community — more a family than a "discussion group" — which for the next week will give each of us a special place within the larger group of five hundred students and adults who are delegates to this Round Square Conference.

The topic today is terrorism. We've just come from a brilliant, if unnerving, lecture by a professor from Harvard who's a leading authority on the subject. So our moderator asks — what do *we* think about what the speaker told us?

One by one, led by the students, the group's members start to speak their minds — and, what's just as important, to listen. In just this manner, the most important business of this or any Round Square Conference — young people forming an interconnection with each other and with adults, in ways which will be both substantive and personal — has begun.

As the days pass, I find myself comparing what I am observing within this little Baraza to the accounts I have heard from adults who, a half-century earlier, witnessed a group of young people connecting with each other during the service project which sparked Round Square's origin. The group process developing here, before my eyes, seems to be just as spontaneous, genuine, and dynamic as what they described. Common ground is being established through shared experience and the discovery of similar hopes and values. Mutual commitments are being expressed, and differences discovered, without the latter being frozen into place by ideological conflict. Each young person is gradually becoming more clearly understood — by others, and by himself or herself, too. Something warmer and more supportive than "tolerance" is growing through this exploration.

Yet what is happening also seems less a fusion of cultures, or a diminishment of real differences, than the creation of a durable *communion amid dissimilarities*. Ideals, hopes, and dreams have been and will continue to be professed and tested. While often congruent, they aren't identical. But *trust* is being established.

I imagine how startling and inspiring the 1954 service project in Greece must have been for the adults who saw and took part in it — and wonder again at how it must have felt to witness that dynamic connection being formed among bold, adventurous young people — youngsters who, like these, had previously known nothing of each other. They too brought much to the encounter — individual promise, sincere generosity, courage, earnestness, and youthful enthusiasm. Even though the process which I am observing is not really a surprise, it is nevertheless thrilling to watch, as these young people reach across personal, national, cultural, and socio-economic barriers — and countless other differences and gaps in understanding — and past doubt, unsureness, and inexperience — to connect, share experiences and adventures, bond, accept, enjoy, and understand. Having seen this happen, not one of the 1954 witnesses was again able (in Hahn's words) to "settle for anything less."

The same kind of inspiring, restorative experience was happening once again, right here at this Conference, for another generation. And for each of us, it will not be easy to emerge unchanged, or to "settle for anything less."

One recalls that the "spark" which began Round Square was kindled not by educational theorists or reformers, but by young people such as these. It's obvious that *the same energy and idealism* exists today within these Round Square delegates.

One should also keep in mind that, moved as they were, the adults who witnessed the 1954 project in Greece were baffled about what needed to happen next, in response to what they had seen. What were they to *do* about that astonishing experience? How could such a revelatory adventure be made to recur, so that its educational power could be sustained, developed, and welded into the fabric of each school, and thereby enrich the education these schools could provide, year after year, to each and every student?

No one has watched the evolution of the Round Square movement and its schools longer, more faithfully, or with more passionate conviction than the Chair of Round Square's Board of Governors, and the organization's Patron, HRH King Constantine of Greece. Himself a graduate of a Round Square school, an Olympic gold medalist in sailing when still a young man, and an exile for decades, the King has been a pillar of Round Square from its first days. He has led scores of meetings of its governing body, and has been an active part of every Conference. His children have been students at (and have exchanged to) Round Square schools. His home has repeatedly been opened to those who work with him to support the movement. King Constantine's belief in the importance of Round Square is at once profound, charismatic, and openly joyful.

We will recall the King's challenge, at the first organizing meeting, to "get on with it!" He has repeatedly worked, both through challenges and an abiding understanding, to help Round Square's evolution occur. He is the sort of skilled, sophisticated, determined, and patient leader every effective organization must have at the head of its governing body.

The two of us met in an unoccupied classroom at Wellington College, a Round Square school in England, just after a Round Square Board meeting had ended. What I sought from King Constantine was his perspective on these decades — a Chair's-eye vision not just of an organization, but of the Round Square *movement*.

In his view, there have been several "turning points" in Round Square's evolution since its early struggles in the 1950's and 60's. Each of these, he said, happened at a moment when the organization "seemed stuck" and was at once under pressure to change, but also to succumb to the anxiety which always seems to be summoned by a call for change.

One such moment, he recalls, happened in 1988, during a Conference at St. Anne's-Windermere School, in England, when it was becoming clear that continued growth in membership would not only replace Round Square's historic character with a less easily imagined "global" identity, but would diminish what until then had been a directive, hands-on role for Heads. The King was under pressure to intervene in this "grow or don't grow" controversy, which had reached a deadlock. In his words, he wanted to "attack" and "break up this log jam." However, he first asked for the advice of a former Round Square governor and trusted friend, Hugh Cavendish. Cavendish suggested that if the King believed in the minds and characters of those who were serving on the Board (then called a "Council"), he might best "step back and wait for a solution to arise."

He did so. A "solution" did emerge, and a commitment to growth was made. "From then on it was clear that we would grow. We would no longer be driven exclusively by Heads, and our identity would be more global. And because of those decisions, we were able to pass Round Square's leadership and governance on to the next generation."

King Constantine suggested that another turning point was the development of Round Square's first Strategic Plan in the 1990's, which again was a step he was happy to encourage, but did not command. While that consensually developed Plan had a broad impact, one aspect which the King feels has proved especially important is that it clarified that "the secretariat and (even more important) the Board would need to evolve with the organization." Roles and responsibilities would be delineated, processes made more open, and channels of communication become more explicit. He has been pleased with the result, not just in relationship to the performance of the expanded secretariat, but in terms of the performance of the governance body. "The Board is starting to really work as a Board." At that moment Round Square's governing body included persons from nine nations. Nevertheless, "nearly every time we meet we have a full house." Unlike many other governing boards of international organizations, Round Square's Board presents a model of good practice; it is a deeply invested group characterized by hard work and responsible, disinterested care.

Where, I asked him, would Round Square be in twenty-five years? In his view, it would *still be changing*. "The only real danger we face isn't related to change, but with getting stale. We have to stay relevant."

Relevant to *what*, I asked? "To the actual lives, hopes, needs and dreams" of students around the world who are involved, was his answer. "The focus of Round Square *always* has to be there. And genuine success must *always* be measured by what students do, what they are becoming."

When a bit later that day I shared the Chairman's vision of the future Round Square with Executive Director Terry Guest, under whose leadership so much progress has been made both by Round Square and its member schools, he wholly concurred — but, as administrators often do, was inclined to set the Board Chair's broad principles within a matrix of detail. For example, he saw Round Square not as "a conventional world organization" but as "a purposeful community of schools and people" — one which would, in another quarter-century, have "grown in a quiet evolution" to something between 100 and 150 member institutions. Yet the Round Square of 2030 which he foresees will be primarily focused on "the same mission as the one which exists today — and that is, *empowering students to be the guardians and leaders of the world.* And it should be added that, by doing this, the individual schools will also be helping one another to be *superb* institutions, not just good ones."

How does Round Square's future look to a somewhat less exalted viewer?, I wondered. I turned to Deerfield's Head of School, the future Headmaster of King's Academy in Jordan, Eric Widmer. Characteristically, Widmer began his answer with a series of questions:

> *Do those who lead and govern Round Square really perceive* ***where*** *it is right now? Do they understand the extraordinary strength of its position, or the scale of its importance? Do they really see where the next challenges will come from?*

These statements were not those of a skeptic, but of a passionate believer. However, they also came from a person who over a long career has acquired a great deal of wisdom about how those who govern a successful organization must maintain a clear vision of that institution in order to maintain its integrity in a changing context.

Widmer's purpose was to stress that Round Square is at once "at a fascinating place in its own evolution, and a fascinating time in history." As he described it, "nations and cultures" have, not entirely of their own volition, been set free from a variety of old constraints. They now find themselves "jockeying for position in the world." And while they are all to a degree aware of "a common destiny of globalism," many are unsure of what that will bring, or what its price may be. At such hinges in history, he said, the characters of those who will lead nations and influence their thinking become critically important.

"We are at a time when schools which want to produce graduates who stand for the right things," schools which are able to help students turn good convictions into an effective foundation for personal actions over a lifetime, will be "very valuable" — both to their own students, and to the world. In Widmer's view, Round Square has the ability to help such schools provide exactly this kind of focus at a critically important time in world history. These schools can thus have an effect on world society which will be far greater than their modest numbers might suggest.

Widmer also saw the globalism-driven spread of English-language instruction as diminishing the importance of Round Square's "Anglophonic nature" as a barrier to membership. That should not imply that language study is becoming less important (Widmer himself was at the time we spoke studying Arabic at his own school) or that, if left alone, Round Square's membership will automatically become more inclusive and global. "There is in fact a greater need for Round Square to be *pro-active* in seeking out new member schools" than in the past, he said. It should be looking in particular for schools which hold similar goals and which, once involved, will be likely to be "confirmed" as invested Round Square institutions through the "rhythm of membership."

Considering the questions Widmer raised, I suspect that what may be even more important than the future evolution of Round Square may be its possible use as a model or template, which could aid the development of new international partnerships among schools.

For instance, consider the possibility of a worldwide alliance in which the working language used by schools and students would be Spanish, rather than English...or, for that matter, Arabic, or French, or Chinese. And what might a multilateral partnership of ambitious *government*-run schools achieve? Many more options are easy to imagine.

It was clear that the educational potential of international networks similar to Round Square was very much on the minds of many in a group of interested educators from several nations who met in February 2005 during a session at an NAIS conference to discuss the Round Square model. Here are a few of the questions asked at that session:

- *How do these programs actually get executed? How does the organization staff, lead, and organize them? How does accountability for all of this work?*

- *We're doing some of this in our school. How do we find partners?*
- *We are exchanging students now, but are frustrated. There's no sense of how to prepare and debrief them, and — particularly — how to help kids "fit back in."*
- *How do you involve a **whole** school, not just a few enthusiasts?*
- *What indicates that a school has reached "the critical mass" of interest that means it's ready to move toward Round Square or a similar partnership?*
- *How can a powerful, but discrete, almost insular service program in a school be "morphed" into something on the scale of Round Square?*
- *How do you pay for all of this?*

Questions such as these aren't reflective of the early stages of inquiry, or of a vague, philosophic interest. Many in the group were obviously well past preliminary thinking. What was being expressed was centered on concrete, practical, immediate issues. These are the kind of questions which are likely to *follow* a decision of principle, and which precede action. Of course, it's too early to predict which (if any) of the schools these speakers represented may actually move ahead toward Round Square membership, or to an adaptation of the Round Square model. But the discussion did make it evident that interest is growing, and at a pace which makes action likely.

§

What's truly unusual about Round Square is that *young people are the power which drives Round Square.* Students are the schools' energizers, visionaries, role models, and in some real ways, their leaders. Round Square's learning consequence flows from this deep, personal, consequential student involvement.

Those who investigate Round Square will discover that the young are not the only people who are transformed by Round Square. Robert Sanderson, 37-year veteran teacher at Ivanhoe Grammar School, in Australia, recently said in his retirement address:

> *There is often a tendency for people to say that the old days are…better than today. This is just not true. And what better illustration than the {Round Square} student presentation we*

saw earlier this evening…

It was the vision of the Principal and the Board to make Ivanhoe a Round Square school…There is no question in my mind that this has produced the greatest cultural change in the School over all these 37 years. I believe that the ideals of the Round Square, with its emphasis on internationalism, understanding and democracy, are going to become…more and more important…important, not just for Ivanhoe, but for all schools that would call themselves 'independent'.

When we talk about promoting cultural change in an organisation, we must understand that this takes a long time to achieve. I have been so impressed by the way the ideals of the Round Square have steadily and surely influenced the members of the School. But the influence is not just to the thinking of everyone involved; it is to their very core. People are now starting to **own** *and to* **live** *these ideals.*

This is vitally important because, in these trying times, our society needs these values more than ever…there can be no greater testimony for what a school really is than this.

—Robert Sanderson

The Round Square organization itself (within each school, and as an international movement) only enables the potential power which young people already possess to be *discovered* by them, to engage with the world in meaningful ways, and to have a consequence. The power that's being tapped is not unique to these youngsters. It slumbers within *all* the world's teenagers. But when enabled to motivate action for human good as is the case at Round Square schools, it can have prodigious results.

As one RS Rep said to me, "Round Square *starts* with kids." Yes. It begins with respect for who they actually are, for their hopes, dreams, and human potential — along with respect for the magnitude and seriousness of the task awaiting these young men and women in the century which is unfolding.

What the study which led to this book taught me is that, if you wish to know and understand Round Square, it is the students at Round Square schools, and those who have graduated and moved on into adult life, whom you must seek out. It is *they* you must listen to as, one by one, they tell you about serving the needs of others, exploring the world, facing up to personal challenges, and — through their own frustrations and failures as well as their successes — learning how to become powerful, effective, and compassionate human beings. It is *their* voices you must heed if you are to grasp Round Square's message.

Young people are the stake-holders who have enabled this multi-school, multi-nation development called Round Square to occur, gain power and credibility, and flourish. It is their worth as human beings, their ability to feel and act on compassion for mankind, and their readiness to work for the betterment of the world, which drives the enterprise.

The purpose of Round Square may indeed be the "empowerment" of the young, as the organization's literature says. However, if you look and listen attentively, these youthful adventurers rarely seem to be in pursuit of something as self-centered as the over-used word "empowerment" might suggest. Rather, what you will observe will be activity which is profoundly altruistic. "Empowerment" may be its long-term consequence, but the immediate drivers are each youngster's hope for the world and his or her capability for compassion.

Offering the young a chance to provide and learn through what has been termed "Samaritan service" was where Round Square began. It is still the most powerful transforming force within the movement.

Kurt Hahn, ever the "founding spirit" of Round Square, expressed that fundamental concept in this way:

> *There are three ways of trying to win the young. There is persuasion, there is compulsion, and there is attraction. You can preach at them; that is a hook without a worm. You can say, "You must volunteer." That is of the devil. And you can tell them, "You are needed."* **That** *appeal hardly ever fails!*

Today, more than ever, *young people need to discover that they are needed*. Round Square merely allows them to glimpse this essential truth, and then gives them a chance to act on that understanding — and to learn through their action.

Appendix A: Additional Resources

Books. While no comprehensive book about Round Square exists other than this one, a brief publication depicts the early history of Round Square as recalled by some who took part in the events of that era. This pamphlet is entitled *Round Square: the Beginnings*, and includes statements by Jocelin Winthrop Young, Roy McComish, and HRH King Constantine. Copies are available through the Round Square office (see below).

Several books are available which focus on a single member school and / or provide biographical information about those who have led them, or who otherwise influenced the development of Round Square and its schools. No doubt more books of this type exist and more will appear; school histories are a fairly usual sort of publication, although in many cases they may not be widely available. The best way to obtain these volumes is to directly contact the Round Square member school in which you have an interest.

Books that I have found particularly valuable include:

Kurt Hahn, an Appreciation of his Life and Work, Ed. David Byatt. Gordonstoun School, Elgin, Scotland, 1976.

Kurt Hahn's Schools and Legacy: to Discover You Can be More and Do More Than You Believed, Martin Flavin. Middle Atlantic Press, Wilmington, Delaware, 1996.

Anthem of Bugles: the Story of Starehe Boys' Centre and School, by Roger Martin. Heinemann Educational Books, Nairobi, 1978.

School Mastery: Straight Talk about Boarding School Management (2nd ed.), Geoffrey Griffin. Lectern Publications, Nairobi, 1996.

The Headmaster: Frank L. Boyden, of Deerfield, John McPhee. Farrar Straus Giroux, New York, 1966.

Frank Boyden of Deerfield; the Vision and Politics of an Educational Idealist, Brian P. Cooke. Madison Books, Lanham, Maryland, 1994.

Deerfield Remembers: a Festschrift for Frank Learoyd Boyden 1902-2002, Ed. Eric Widmer. Deerfield Academy Press, Deerfield, Massachusetts, 2004.

Gordonstoun: Ancient Estate and Modern School (2nd ed.), Henry L. Brereton. Gordonstoun School, Elgin, Scotland, 1982.

Outward Bound USA: Learning through Experience in Adventure-Based Education, Joshua L. Miner and Joe Boldt. William Morrow and Co., New York, 1981.

Timbertop: an Innovation in Australian Education, E.H. Montgomery and J. R. Darling. F. W. Cheshire, Melbourne, 1967.

Research Papers / Dissertations: Several academic studies have examined Round Square and / or its schools. Two notable examples are:

Day, J.H. (1980). *The Basic Conception of Education of Kurt Hahn and its Translation into Practice.* (A thesis submitted in fulfillment of the requirements for the degree of Master of Education, University of Queensland, Australia).

Redler, P.J. [2003]. *Educational Leadership in the Organisation. How Effective is it and What Needs Reforming?* [Southport: The Southport School, Australia].

Archival Materials. There are two useful, professionally maintained archives of documents (graphic materials as well as textual archives) which contain records relating to the history of Round Square. These archives, which in each case are sections of larger libraries, are located at Schüle Schloss Salem in Germany, and at Gordonstoun School, in Scotland. Contact information:

Ms. Sophie Weidlich, Archivist
    Schüle Schloss Salem
    Salem College, Schloss Spetzgart
    D-88662 Ueberlingen, Germany

Mr. Alan Wills, Archivist
    Gordonstoun School
    Elgin, Morayshire
    Scotland 1V30 5RF

Current Information. The most easily accessible source of up-to-date information about Round Square, its ongoing and projected activities, and its schools, is the Round Square website: www.roundsquare.org.

    A variety of printed materials, videotapes / CDs, newsletters and other information are available from the Round Square international office. Directions for reaching this office or the Executive Director by post, email or telephone are posted on the website.

Appendix B: Teaching Character, Judgment, and Courage

The following is adapted by permission from an address given by HRH Prince Andrew, The Duke of York, at a National Association of Independent Schools Conference in San Francisco, California, USA, in March 2002. I am most grateful to Prince Andrew for permitting this adaptation to be made and included in this volume. — PT

I happily went to Gordonstoun, a school steeped in its original ethos of preparing future leaders [by engaging] the whole person, and not just the mind.

I well remember the initial feelings of how responsibility rests on your shoulders when it is first given you. I also well remember the self admonishment of failing, and then of succeeding in shouldering that responsibility. The knowledge of failure gave rise to even greater understanding of how to succeed. When you are put in charge of a crew of a cutter, as I was in seamanship classes, the frustration of not being able to get this unruly lot of individuals to work as a team was paramount. We were [at first] not able to get our boat out of the harbour without being helped by the seamanship staff to regain order from chaos!

Initially, I wasn't particularly inspired at Gordonstoun. I went with the flow and didn't get into much trouble; in fact I just blended in with the crowd for the first few years there.

That lack of inspiration lasted until, by chance, I was assigned the next door locker to a young man who was on a Round Square exchange from Canada. This young man was remarkable, as he helped me to be introduced to international understanding and to a chance to accept challenge that was outside my comfort zone.

This was the very inspiration that I had needed. I begged and cajoled my parents to allow me to go to his school, Lakefield College School, as a Round Square exchange student, in order to experience this challenge first hand.

So, on a very cold day in early January, 1977, I arrived in Canada to begin my first international experience. Talk about being a fish out of water, and at the same time in way over my head! But I spent the next nine months in Canada at this school, and was inspired beyond anything I had imagined might happen. It is a memory which lasts to this day. And it is largely due to that single experience that I am here today.

Most of us go through very few life changing experiences. I have been fortunate in some ways and unfortunate in others, and have had more than my fair share. But the Lakefield exchange was the most influential for my future, probably because it was the first. Since that time at Lakefield I have remained in close touch with the school and served for a number of years as an active board member. So — I know and understand the foibles of North American education, particularly in the independent sector.

But my purpose is not telling my own history. I want to stir debate about a few issues which my history has clarified for me, and which might be facing you today and in the future.

The first of these is how teamwork and leadership may be taught and learned. It doesn't matter what career a student chooses; at some stage, he or she is going to be a part of a team, working closely together to reach a goal. Someone is going to have to lead that team and have an understanding of how to engage the team in achieving its goal. This cannot be taught in the classroom with sufficient vigor. We don't learn by being told to lead. We as a species can only learn the arts of teamwork and leadership through experience, which must include failure as well as success.

I believe that the earlier a person understands the principles of teamwork, communication and leadership, the greater chance he or she will have of succeeding in the wider, crueller world after school. And don't let us forget — the principle of education is to instill the ability to *learn* — not to be taught.

Fundamental to teaching teamwork and leadership is making purposefully directed experience a part of a whole education. (This understanding is the common strand linking Round Square and Outward Bound.) The educator's responsibility is not to just instruct the young, but to "impel each one into experience." The essential word is the verb. Ordinary experience is universal; but "impelled" experience can be part of a powerful instructive design. And the "impelling" we are talking about isn't just pushing — it is directed, purposeful pushing. There is all the difference in the world between "impelling" and just placing your boot on a young person's derriere and giving the tyke a shove.

Much the same thing can be done, of course, with "impelled" learning through service, or through international work. Each can lead to a changed, more realistic, more committed, and more prepared adult view of the world, and of oneself. Such lessons may not be of small importance if the specific young people involved are those attending NAIS schools in the USA. They are likely to disproportionately impact human society and the planet during the 21st century.

Each of us now realizes that the world is different to that preceding September 11, 2001. You as educators should be asking how you can give your students the clearest view of their real responsibilities in a post-9/11 world society.

I would propose that one part of the educational tool kit at your disposal could, if used and used properly, help these young people attain a greater understanding of teamwork, leadership, and communication with each other, and also help them better understand failure. It is only through understanding our mistakes that we can learn and become something we had not previously realiised was possible.

Apart from the capability of the individual human being, the single most important factor in any form of work and service environment is leadership. Leadership ultimately determines if an organization succeeds or fails. When strategies, processes or cultures must change, the key to successful change is leadership.

Effective leadership is the function of three personality traits: personal character, judgement, and courage. Most people will tell you that they want their leaders to be visionary and give direction, but they must first be steadfast, trustworthy, and optimistically honest.

School should introduce each student to the art of leadership. In other words, each student should be given the opportunity to experience responsibility. This should not be just dumped on him or her, but should be learnt through small experiences of teamwork, so small at first that the student might not even realize he is leading. The art, for the educator, is to find these opportunities, give them with supervision, and move along toward an objective where the student can assume leadership on his own.

Failures are an essential part of this learning process. The process of picking yourself up, brushing yourself off, and starting all over again is as instructive and valuable as the experience of triumph.

One's "comfort zone" does not accept failure, nor does it welcome new types of challenge. When I went to Lakefield I was moving well beyond that comfort zone. I was faced with a completely different culture and lifestyle than what I was used to in the UK. I was given opportunities and challenges I never realised were possible, and began to set myself goals without knowing it. Before long, I spent a night out in a snow hole in just a sleeping bag, in seriously minus temperatures. Later I ran a half marathon. I am *not* a runner, but I was determined to complete this. I did, — and I can promise you, never again! But it did serve a useful lesson. In my mind I now knew that I'd done it once, and could do it or something similar again.

A Lakefield canoe expedition in the Arctic definitely took me even farther out of my comfort zone. To succeed, we needed to work as a team, both within our canoes and as a part of the whole expedition. We trained hard, worked together, accepted the risks, and were rewarded at the end with a feeling of complete euphoria. The canoe experience proved particularly valuable to me in later life. As a Navy helicopter pilot, I worked with a second crewman beside me in the aircraft. We were a team. We not only had to fly together but use the aircraft and our skills together, as a single tool. I had done it all before, in different circumstances but with similar results — in a canoe.

Another aspect of educating the whole person involves integrating service into the curriculum. Every student should taste the experience of giving his or her time and effort to others who are in need. A school is not only an excellent place for young people to learn about social responsibility through service, but is usually in an good position in its community to provide some the of the services which are really needed. These need not only involve welfare and support work, but can include the provision of rescue and emergency service for the surrounding area. Service work of this kind allows students to be genuinely needed, even if they are called on at times which might be considered inconvenient by them, such as on weekends or during the evenings.

The schools in Round Square will argue that when voluntary service takes students not just beyond the school but away from both home and country, it can also get students away from their pre-conceived ideas about other countries, their own homeland, and themselves. International service becomes a concrete basis for seeing, breathing and feeling another life and culture than one's own. The point is not only that the student can give something to those living in a developing nation, but he or she can also learn deeply about that place and its people, and about herself or himself through living and working in a place which is unfamiliar, and may at first be uncomfortable. This type of learning requires teamwork and leadership, too, as these are usually necessary to reach the goals of any service project.

The benefit of challenging service to students can be life-changing, and it can powerfully advance understanding of international concerns and issues. Surely this is important at a time when there is so much misunderstanding and mistrust in the world.

So, as you can see, I was extremely fortunate in my schooling. I was given the chance to work in a team, both as a member and as a leader. I was given responsibility at an early age, and I began to understand its gravity. And I was lucky enough to experience another country and school when this had much to teach me. I feel tremendously grateful.

As we enter this 21st century, the breadth of knowledge and inspiration you instill in your students can have a lasting and most likely disproportionate effect. Leadership, service, and international understanding are three of the vital keys to helping your students make the uncertain future that's outside your gates a good one for themselves, and the world. I wish you well in this awesome task!

Appendix C: Contributors

The following persons spoke with me about Round Square during the writing of this book. They are listed alphabetically, without distinction as to whether an individual is a student, graduate, staff member, school head, governor, or a Round Square official. School names are abbreviated.

To each and every one of those whose names are on this list, my deepest thanks! *You* made my own Round Square experience a wonderful and rewarding adventure! I hope this book lives up to your expectations.

Joshua Abaki, *Starehe*
Nicola Abernethy, *St. Cyprian's*
Walter Abila, *Starehe*
Ivanka Acquisto, *St. Stithian's*
Pratik Agarwala, *Welham*
Miriam Al Ali, *Salem*
Lilly Alexander, *St. Philip's*
Felix Allsop, *St. Philip's*
Patrick Amor, *Athenian*
Ria-Maree Anzolin, *St. Philip's*
Ashley Argoon, *Billanook*
Mary Armstrong, *Salem*
Colin Armstrong, *Athenian*
Kanti Bajpai, *Doon*
Wafula Gilbert Barasa, *Starehe*
Megan Barber, *St. Cyprian's*
Prabir Basu, *Welham*
Sahil Kumar Batta, *Doon*
Nikhil Bector, *Doon*
Chris Beeson, *Athenian*
Jeannine Bell, *Athenian*
Lara Beltrame, *Ivanhoe*
Kim Bennett, *St. Philip's*
Amy Bennett, *St. Cyprian's*
Carlo Berardi, *Gordonstoun*
Jessica Bernon, *St. Stithian's*
Silas Bett, *Starehe*
Cecile Bezuidenhoudt, *St. Stithian's*
Charles Bierk, *Lakefield*
Jamie Bignell, *Lakefield*
Virginia Birrell, *Ivanhoe*
Catherine Blais, *Appleby*
Hannah Blake, *Billanook*
Jenica Blondeel, *St. Stithian's*
Megan Bobos, *St. Philip's*
Mitchell Bodycoat, *Ivanhoe*
Alex Bolzan, *Ivanhoe*
Emma-Lee Bourne, *Mowbray*
Arnie Boyle, *Lakefield*
Dick Bradford, *Athenian*
Manuela Bregar, *Ivanhoe*
Anne Bremicker, *Salem*
Frances Briggs, *St. Cyprian's*
Dyke Brown, *Athenian*
Michael Brown, *Billanook*
Joan Buckley, *St. Stithian's*
Bernhard Bueb, *Salem*
Jess Bunting, *St. Philip's*
Richard Burge, *St. Stithian's*
Valerie Burrus, *Gordonstoun*
Charles Butcher, *St. Philip's*
Sipho Buys, *St. Stithian's*
David Byatt, *Gordonstoun*
Rebecca Byrnes, *St. Philip's*
Natalie Calder, *Ballarat*
Alyce Caldwell, *Stanford Lake*
Rhiannon Carman, *Billanook*
Ella Carmichael, *St. Philip's*
David Carr, *St. Cyprian's*
Danielle Carstens, *St. Stithian's*
Martin Cayouette, *Lakefield*
Jacqui Chlanda, *St. Philip's*
Katie Chodak, *Salem*
Maggie Chodak, *Salem*
Jaewon Choi, *Deerfield*
Ashish Choudhary, *Welham*
Aninda Choudhary, *Welham*
Sarah Chow, *Deerfield*
Jontae Clapp, *Athenian*
Killian Clarke, *Deerfield*
Caitlin Clarke, *Deerfield*
Ashlee Clough, *Mowbray*
Kate Coughlan, *Ballarat*
Tim Cole, *Ballarat*
Peter Cole, *Ballarat*
Lauren Coleman, *St. Philip's*
Olivia Collie, *Gordonstoun*
Mitch Conelly, *Billanook*
HM King Constantine, *Round Square*
Julia Conway, *Deerfield*

Sara Cooper, *Lakefield*
Maxine Craker, *St. Philip's*
Mackenzie Crawford, *Lakefield*
Nina Crawley, *Billanook*
Tercia da Silva, *Stanford Lake*
Talia da Silva, *Stanford Lake*
Gabriella da Silva, *St. Stithian's*
Michael Daffy, *St. Philip's*
Arielle Dalle, *Lakefield*
Libby Dalrymple, *Lakefield*
Eleanor Dase, *Athenian*
Steve & Joanna Davenport, *Athenian*
Bryn Davies, *Mowbray*
Janetta Davis, *Mowbray*
Ben Davis, *St. Philip's*
Brian Dawson, *Stanford Lake*
Taryn de Beer, *St. Stithian's*
Thandi de Wit, *St. Cyprian's*
Matt DeRemer, *Ivanhoe*
Ryan DeRemer, *Ivanhoe*
Pushparaj Deshpande, *Doon*
Anthea Dickson, *St. Stithian's*
Carl Jobst Diesterweg, *Gordonstoun*
Elena Dimolarova, *Salem*
Tess Dolan, *Billanook*
Zoe Donovan, *St. Philip's*
Katharina Dragon, *Salem*
Freanna Drew, *St. Philip's*
Leon Gazet du Chattelier, *St. Stithian's*
Tessa Fairbairn, *St. Cyprian's*
Jett Fein, *Deerfield*
Kale Fein, *Deerfield*
Lutz Fells, *Salem*
Oliver Field, *St. Stithian's*
Annabel Fleming-Brown, *Gordonstoun*
Megan Fortington, *Billanook*
Andrew Fox, *Ivanhoe*
Emma Fraser, *Mowbray*
Rod Fraser, *Ivanhoe*
Sarah Freeman, *Lakefield*
Stevie Jane French, *St. Stithian's*
Adilya Gaddh, *Welham*
Jeffifer Gassowski, *Appleby*
Patrick Gatonga, *Starehe*
Julia Sophie Geissler, *Salem*
Harry Gow, *Gordonstoun*
Lisa Gray, *Billanook*
Geoffrey Griffin, *Starehe*

Gillian Grossman, *Deerfield*
Terry & Sue Guest, *Round Square*
Rebecca Guyon, *Athenian*
Katharina Barbara Haack, *Salem*
Leanne Hablutzel, *St. Cyprian's*
Stephanie Haggett, *St. Philip's*
John Hamilton, *Gordonstoun*
Xenia Hawrylyshyn, *Appleby*
Jackie Hawthrey, *St. Cyprian's*
Louise Hayward, *St. Cyprian's*
Lydia Hemphill, *Deerfield*
Lauren Hicks, *St. Philip's*
Stephen Higgs, *Ballarat*
Ed Hill, *Gordonstoun*
Jared Hill, *Billanook*
Asta Hill, *St. Philip's*
Karima Hirji, *Gordonstoun*
Linda Horn, *Salem*
Claire Howan, *St. Stithian's*
Felice Howden, *Mowbray*
Jason Hreha, *Athenian*
Kodie Hultgren, *Billanook*
Daniel Ionnidis, *Ivanhoe*
Timothy Ischia, *Billanook*
Meagan Jacobs, *St. Philip's*
Brooke Jan, *Lakefield*
Stephanie Jearey, *St. Stithian's*
Renate Johnny, *St. Philip's*
Lia Johnson-Strike, *St. Philip's*
Annabel Johnson-Teal, *Gordonstoun*
Lindsay Joseph, *Lakefield*
Sudipt Junija, *Welham*
Dalip Singh Kang, *Doon*
Wilson Kanyi, *Starehe*
Pranavakshar Kapur, *Doon*
Peter Kariuki, *Deerfield*
Alex Karolas, *Ivanhoe*
Akhil Kejriwal, *Doon*
Elizabeth Kelly, *St. Cyprian's*
Sarah Kerr, *St. Stithian's*
Wendy & Bertie Kerr, *St. Stithian's*
Jared Kettle, *Billanook*
Marij Khan, *Welham*
Faroz Nath Khosla, *Doon*
John Paul Kibet, *Starehe*
Esther Kim, *Appleby*
Charles Gitau Kimani, *Starehe*
Sammy Kimutai, *Starehe*

Gina King, *St. Cyprian's*
Yume Kobayashi, *Salem*
Teri Kopa, *St. Philip's*
Jaymie Kourlinis, *Ivanhoe*
Udit Kumar, *Welham*
Tushaar Kuthiala, *Doon*
Jayant Lal, *Doon*
Karam Vir Lamba, *Doon*
Emma Lambie, *Gordonstoun*
Justus Lando, *Starehe*
Sonia Lazar, *Ivanhoe*
Paul Jisas Lemasagarai, *Starehe*
Ian Lerner, *Gordonstoun*
Richard Life, *Lakefield*
Adam Livori, *Ivanhoe*
Emily Lockett, *St. Philip's*
James Ebenyo Lodunga, *Starehe*
Stephen Lowry, *St. Stithian's*
Martha Lyman, *Deerfield*
Friedrich Magalhaes, *Salem*
Amay Malik, *Doon*
Munir Malik-Noor, *Appleby*
Merryn Manley, *St. Stithian's*
Alasdair Martin, *St. Stithian's*
Pheladi Mathabatha, *Stanford Lake*
Nikiwe Matukane, *St. Stithian's*
Lindsay McClelland, *Athenian*
Alec McCubbin, *Lakefield*
Rob McGuiness, *Appleby*
Francesca McKenzie, *Athenian*
Elle McLachlan, *Ballarat*
Ian & Elaine McLachlan, *St. Stithian's*
Guy & Joanne McLean, *Appleby*
Fiona McNestry, *Lakefield*
Tatjana Meirelles, *St. Cyprian's*
Kelsey Middleton, *St. Philip's*
Maanda Milubi, *Stanford Lake*
Reena Mohan, *Appleby*
Lillian Molakeng, *St. Cyprian's*
Jacqui Molotsane, *St. Stithian's*
Laaika Moosa, *Stanford Lake*
Angus Morina, *St. Philip's*
Kirsten Mortimer, *St. Stithian's*
Gemma Mostran, *St. Philip's*
Christopher Moyses, *St. Philip's*
Joseph Mugisha, *Starehe*
Stephen Mulder, *St. Stithian's*
Laura Mullin, *Gordonstoun*

Kate Mumme, *Billanook*
Katharina Mybes, *Salem*
Christopher Myers, *St. Philip's*
Peter Ndungu, *Starehe*
Alex Nebesar, *Athenian*
Chalie Nejedly, *Athenian*
Ulrike Niederhofer, *Salem*
Anthony Kimani Njoroge, *Starehe*
Kristian North, *Gordonstoun*
K. Ninakhulu Ntsanwisi, *Stanford Lake*
John O'Shea, *Mowbray*
Jack Obaro, *Starehe*
Olufunke Ogunkoya, *Gordonstoun*
Ngozi Ojukwu, *Athenian*
Vincent Odongo Okumu, *Starehe*
Loiton Joseph Otieno, *Starehe*
Hesbon Owino Oundo, *Starehe*
Tamara Owen, *St. Stithian's*
Bridget Painter, *Stanford Lake*
Vishnu Painuli, *Welham*
Tegan Pannell, *St. Philip's*
Parth Parasher, *Welham*
Elishia Parry, *Mowbray*
Ione Paterson, *Gordonstoun*
Sue Patterson, *Mowbray*
Steve Pessegueiro, *Stanford Lake*
Josh Philip, *Ivanhoe*
Amitav Philip, *Doon*
Dieter Plate, *Salem*
Sarah Pollitt, *St. Philip's*
Alex Pollitt, *St. Cyprian's*
Bronwyn Pope, *St. Stithian's*
Kiara Price, *St. Philip's*
Raghav Puri, *Doon*
Brooke Puttergill, *St. Stithian's*
Mark & Jenny Pyper, *Gordonstoun*
Hayley Quick, *Billanook*
Gulab & Ratna Ramchandani, *Doon*
Mmanake Rathete, *Stanford Lake*
Bridgette Raynolds-Perry, *Athenian*
Jack Read, *Ivanhoe*
Pierina Redler, *Southport*
Gemma Reece, *Billanook*
Leanne Reed, *Stanford Lake*
Olivia Rejniak, *Appleby*
Liana Renden, *Ballarat*
Diane Rogers, *Lakefield*
Tamlyn Roman, *St. Cyprian's*

Alan Ross, *Billanook*
Karl Roth, *Salem*
Keeba Roy, *Gordonstoun*
Tia Saley, *Lakefield*
Navjeet Sandhu, *Appleby*
Madhav Saraswat, *Doon*
Jeremy Sasson, *Athenian*
Alessandro Scalca, *St. Stithian's*
Kendra Schindler, *St. Philip's*
Sara Schlabsz, *St. Philip's*
Emma Schubert, *St. Philip's*
Sophia Schwan, *Salem*
Clancy Scollay, *St. Philip's*
Chelsea Scott, *Stanford Lake*
Jamie Scott, *Stanford Lake*
Emma Seager, *Lakefield*
Vious Sehgal, *Doon*
Erika Semmens, *Gordonstoun*
Arun Sharma, *Welham*
Kate Shiller, *St. Stithian's*
Mohit Krishna Shrestha, *Welham*
Myles Sigelsma, *Ivanhoe*
Luke Simmends, *St. Stithian's*
Brian Simons, *Mowbray*
Aftab Singh, *Welham*
Apoorv Singh, *Welham*
Shivtaj Singh, *Doon*
Pulkit Singhania, *Welham*
Darren Smith, *Appleby*
Hollie Smith, *Billanook*
Brodie Smith, *Billanook*
David Smith, *St. Stithian's*
Louise Smith, *St. Stithian's*
Emma Smith, *St. Cyprian's*
Jarryd Solomon, *Billanook*
Paul Sprenger, *St. Stithian's*
Niki Stefanelli, *Athenian*
Tim Steinecke, *Salem*
Ryan Stevens, *Ivanhoe*
Sive Stofile, *St. Cyprian's*
Caroline Strauss, *St. Stithian's*
Charles Straut, *Deerfield*
Monica Streifer, *Athenian*
Andre Strydom, *St. Stithian's*
Lucy Stuart-Clark, *St. Cyprian's*
Martin Kelly Suku, *Starehe*
Rod Summerton, *Ivanhoe*
Tom Swope, *Athenian*

Nathalie Thierjung, *Salem*
Sarah Thomas, *St. Cyprian's*
Allison Thompson, *Appleby*
Steve Tindall, *St. Stithian's*
Jon-Marc Tomlinson, *St. Stithian's*
Matthew Townshend, *St. Stithian's*
Justine Tribe, *St. Cyprian's*
Chris Tudor, *St. Philip's*
Hannah Tunley, *Ivanhoe*
Arlene Ustin, *Athenian*
Brittany Van Heugten, *St. Philip's*
Mishal Verjee, *Lakefield*
Kathryn Vickery, *St. Cyprian's*
Ankit Vinaik, *Welham*
Anna-Marie von Mangoldt, *Salem*
Silas Wafula, *Starehe*
Sidharth Wahi, *Doon*
George Gathuru Waithaka, *Starehe*
Jenn Wallace, *St. Cyprian's*
Olivia Walton, *Gordonstoun*
Sophie Weidlich, *Salem*
Ann West, *Round Square*
Laura Wheatley, *St. Philip's*
Helen White, *Salem*
Eric Widmer, *Deerfield*
Richard Wilkinson, *St. Stithian's*
Jess Williams, *St. Stithian's*
Timothy Willis, *St. Stithian's*
Michael Willson, *Stanford Lake*
Jocelin Winthrop Young, *Round Square*
Frances Wolfaardt, *St. Cyprian's*
Leala Wong, *Lakefield*
Emily Zalewski, *Athenian*

Appendix D: Survey Form

Round Square Student / Graduate Questionnaire

All current or former students at Round Square Schools are invited to complete this questionnaire, which will be used in preparing a forthcoming book about Round Square.

You may provide your response online, by copying the survey form, adding responses, and pasting it into an email to be sent to {p_tacy@caisct.org} or by printing a copy, completing it, and mailing it to Questionnaire, c/o P. Tacy, 8 Ivy Rd., Mystic, CT 06355 USA.

Surveys must be received by March 31, 2005. Please answer each question as honestly as possible. Do NOT include your name or the name of your school. Thank you!!

General

I am	○ a student at	○ a graduate of a Round Square school.
My age is	○ under 20	○ 20-29 ○ 30 and over
I am	○ male	○ female

Part I

Directions: *please mark / underline the number which best indicates how strongly you agree / disagree with each statement.*

• Giving my time and resources to help others is important to me, and will continue to be important.

Agree   ○ 1   ○ 2   ○ 3   ○ 4   ○ 5   ○ 6   ○ 7   Disagree

• If my generation does the right things, we CAN provide a better life for the world's people.

Agree   ○ 1   ○ 2   ○ 3   ○ 4   ○ 5   ○ 6   ○ 7   Disagree

• Every person has a responsibility to stand up for what is right and good, even if doing so might expose that person to unpopularity or risk.

Agree   ○ 1   ○ 2   ○ 3   ○ 4   ○ 5   ○ 6   ○ 7   Disagree

- I am confident that I have the basic skills and courage I will need to serve and lead others.

Agree ○ 1 ○ 2 ○ 3 ○ 4 ○ 5 ○ 6 ○ 7 Disagree

- Being well educated makes a person more valuable to the world than other people.

Agree ○ 1 ○ 2 ○ 3 ○ 4 ○ 5 ○ 6 ○ 7 Disagree

- Every human being has a responsibility for the protection of the global environment.

Agree ○ 1 ○ 2 ○ 3 ○ 4 ○ 5 ○ 6 ○ 7 Disagree

- I believe it is important for all of us to think of ourselves as citizens of the world, not merely as citizens of our own nations.

Agree ○ 1 ○ 2 ○ 3 ○ 4 ○ 5 ○ 6 ○ 7 Disagree

- Each person has an obligation to understand and feel compassion for others, even those who hold very different views and beliefs.

Agree ○ 1 ○ 2 ○ 3 ○ 4 ○ 5 ○ 6 ○ 7 Disagree

- It is important that a Round Square experience require a student to confront the possibility of failure as well as an opportunity for success.

Agree ○ 1 ○ 2 ○ 3 ○ 4 ○ 5 ○ 6 ○ 7 Disagree

- I now know that I can accomplish much more with my life than I had once thought possible.

Agree ○ 1 ○ 2 ○ 3 ○ 4 ○ 5 ○ 6 ○ 7 Disagree

Part 2

*Briefly describe **one specific experience** you had as a result of a Round Square program or activity. (Possible examples might be an experience during a service project, or at a conference, during an expedition, or as the result of a student exchange which sent you to another school or brought someone from another school to live / work with you). Be sure to explain **what** happened, **why** this experience was important for you, and **what you learned** from it.*

Round Square Schools, 2006

The following schools were Round Square Members at the time this book went to press in July 2006. Other schools (not listed) were Regional Members of Round Square organizations or were active applicants for Membership. Still more had expressed interest in obtaining Membership or were becoming involved in Round Square activities. For all these reasons, this is a list that is bound to become incomplete long before the book itself is likely to be reprinted.

Happily, fully accurate information will always be at hand. Current illustrations for this volume will always be posted on-line at http://www.roundsquare.org/idealsatwork.htm.

An up to date online list of Member schools can be found at
http://www.roundsquare.org/members.htm.

Abbotsholme School
Staffordshire, England
Coed – Day / Boarding
273 Students – Ages 4 to 18
Founded 1889 — RS 1985
www.abbotsholme.com

Aiglon College
Villars, Switzerland
Coed – Boarding / Day
350 Students – Ages 9 to 18
Founded 1949 — RS 1967
www.aiglon.ch

Appleby College
Oakville, ON, Canada
Coed – Day / Boarding
687 Students – Ages 11 to 18
Founded 1911 — RS 1992
www.appleby.on.ca

The Armidale School
Armidale, NSW, Australia
Boys – Day / Boarding
560 Students – Ages 4 to 18
Founded 1889 — RS 1996
www.as.edu.au

The Athenian School
Danville, CA, U.S.A.
Coed – Day / Boarding
449 Students – Ages 14 – 19
Founded 1965 — RS Founder
www.athenian.org

Ballarat Grammar School
Wendouree, Victoria, Australia
Coed — Day / Boarding
1100 Students – Ages 5 to 18
Founded 1975 — RS 1996
www.bgs.vic.edu.au

Baylor School
Chattanooga, TN, USA
Coed – Day / Boarding
1076 Students – Ages 12 to 18
Founded 1893 — RS 2003
www.baylorschool.org

Bayview Glen
Toronto, ON, Canada
Co-ed – Day
991 Students – Ages 2 to 18
Founded 1962 — RS 2001
www.bvg.on.ca

Bermuda High School for Girls
Pembroke Parish, Bermuda
Girls – Day
350 Students – Ages 11 to 18
Founded 1894 — RS 2005
www.bhs.bm

Billanook College
Melbourne, Australia
Coed – Day
880 Students – Ages 6 to 18
Founded 1980 — RS 1991
www.billanook.vic.edu.au

Birklehof Schüle
Hinterzarten, Germany
Coed – Day / Boarding
210 Students – Ages 10 to 20
Founded 1932 — RS 1987
www.birklehof.de

Bishop's College School
Lennoxville, QC, Canada
Coed – Day / Boarding
259 Students – Ages 12 to 19
Founded 1836 — RS 1986
www.bishopscollegeschool.com

Box Hill School
Surrey, England
Coed – Day / Boarding
350 Students – Ages 11 to 19
Founded 1959 — RS Founder
www.boxhillschool.org.uk

Cobham Hall
Kent, England
Girls – Day / Boarding
218 Students – Ages 11 to 18
Founded 1962 — RS 1968
www.cobhamhall.com

Collingwood School
West Vancouver, B.C., Canada
Coed – Day
1188 Students – Ages 5 to 18
Founded 1984 — RS 1998
www.collingwood.org

Daly College
Indore, India
Coed – Day / Boarding
1768 Students — Ages 3 to 18
Founded 1882 — RS 2005
www.dalycollege.org

Deerfield Academy
Deerfield, MA, USA
Coed – Boarding / Day
604 Students – Ages 13 to 19
Founded 1797 — RS 2001
www.deerfield.edu

The Doon School
Dehradun INDIA
Boys – Boarding
512 Students – Ages 12 to 17
Founded 1935 — RS1981
www.doonschool.com

Ermitage, Ecole Internationale de France (l'Ermitage)
Maisons Laffitte, France
Coed – Day / Boarding
910 Students – Ages 3 – 17
Founded 1941 — RS 2005
www.ermitage.fr

Glenlyon Norfolk School
Victoria B.C., Canada
Coed – Day
666 Students – Ages 4 - 18
Founded 1912 — RS1997
www.GlenlyonNorfolk.bc.ca

Gordonstoun School
Moray, Scotland
Coed – Boarding / Day
456 Students – Ages 13 to 18
Founded 1933 — RS Founder
www.gordonstoun.org.uk

Hellenic College London
London, England
Coed – Day
95 Students – Ages 2 - 16
Founded — RS 1996
www.hellenic.org.uk

The Hotchkiss School
Lakeville, CT, USA
Coed – Boarding / Day
566 Students – Ages 14 to 18
Founded 1891 — RS 2004
www.hotchkiss.org

The Indian School
Muscat, Oman
Coed – Day
1,739 Students – Ages 3 to 18
Founded 1990 — RS 1996
www.indianschool.com

Ivanhoe Grammar School
Ivanhoe, Victoria, Australia
Coed — Day
1100 Students — Ages 11 to 18
Founded 1915 — RS 1996
www.igs.vic.edu.au

Lakefield College School
Lakefield, ON, Canada
Coed – Boarding / Day
359 Students – Ages 12 to 18
Founded 1879 — RS 1978
www.lakefieldcs.on.ca

Stiftung Louisenlund
Gueby, Germany
Coed – Day/Boarding
369 Students – Ages 10 – 19
Founded 1949 — RS 1978
www.louisenlund.de

Markham College
Lima, Peru
Coed – Day
1,874 Students – Ages 4 to 18
Founded 1946 — RS 2004
www.markham.edu.pe

Maru A Pula
Gaborone, Botswana
Coed – Day / Boarding
580 Students – Ages 12 – 19
Founded 1972 — RS 1999
www.map.ac.bw

Mayo College
Rajasthan, India
Boys – Day / Boarding
814 Students – Ages 9 – 17
Founded 1869 — RS 2003
www.mayocollege.com

Mowbray College
Melton, Victoria, Australia
Coed — Day
1,424 Students – Ages 5 to 18
Founded 1983 — RS 1997
www.mowbray.vic.edu.au

The Regent's School
Banglamung, Chonburi, Thailand
Coed – Day/Boarding
780 Students – Ages 2 to 18
Founded 1995 — RS 2001
www.regents.ac.th

Schüle Schloss Salem
Salem, Germany
Coed – Boarding / Day
580 Students – Ages 10 to 19
Founded 1920 — RS Founder
www.salemcollege.de

The Scindia School
Gwalior, Madhya Pradesh, India
Boys – Boarding
600 Students – Ages 10 to 17
Founded 1897 — RS 1990
www.scindia.edu

Sedbergh School
Montebello, QC, Canada
Coed – Boarding / Day
100 students – Ages 10 to 18
Founded 1939 — RS 1987
www.sedbergh.com

The Southport School
Southport, Queensland, Australia
Boys – Day / Boarding
1,310 Students – Ages 5 to 18
Founded 1901 — RS 1973
www.tss.qld.edu.au

St. Andrew's College
Christchurch, New Zealand
Coed – Day / Boarding
1,308 Students – Ages 5 to 20
Founded 1917 — RS 2003
www.stac.school.nz

St. Clement's School
Toronto, ON Canada
Girls – Day
425 Students – Ages 5 to 17
Founded 1901 — RS 2002
www.scs.on.ca

St. Cyprians School
Cape Town, South Africa
Girls – Day
708 Students – Ages 3 to 18
Founded 1871 — RS 1998
www.stcyprian's.co.za

St. Philip's College
Alice Springs, NT, Australia
Coed – Day / Boarding
610 Students – Ages 12 to 18
Founded — RS 1996
www.stphilips.nt.edu.au

St. Stithian's Boys' College
Randburg, Gauteng, South Africa
Boys — Day
770 Students — Ages 14 to 18
Founded 1953 — RS 1998
www.stithian.com

St. Stithian's Girls' College
Randburg, Gauteng, South Africa
Girls — Day
475 Students — Ages 13 to 18
Founded 1953 — RS 1999
www.stithian.com

Stanford Lake College
Haenertsburg, South Africa
Coed – Boarding / Day
268 Students – Ages 13 to 18
Founded 1998 — RS 2003
www.stanfordlakecollege.co.za

Stanstead College
Stanstead, QC, Canada
Coed – Boarding / Day
223 Students – Ages 12 to 18
Founded 1872 — RS 2002
www.stansteadcollege.com

Starehe Boys' Centre & School
Nairobi, Kenya
Boys – Boarding / Day
1050 students – Ages 14 to 19
Founded 1959 — RS 1989
stareheboyscentre.org /
www.starehe.net.com

Tamagawa Gakuen
Machida, Tokyo, Japan
Coed – Day
3,045 Students – Ages 3 to 18
Founded 1929 — RS 2005
www.tamagawa.jp

Tiger Kloof Educational Institution
Vryburg, North West Province, South Africa
Coed – Day / Boarding
383 Students – Ages 13 to 18
Founded 1904 — RS 2000
www.tigerkloof.nw.school.za

Trinity Anglican School
Cairns, Queensland, Australia
Coed – Day
1,148 Students – Ages Prep – Year 12
Founded 1982 — RS 2004
www.tas.qld.edu.au

Vidya Devi Jindal School
Hissar, Haryana, India
Girls – Boarding / Day
868 Students – Ages 8 to 18
Founded 1984 — RS 2004
www.vdjs.org

Vivek High School
Chandigarh, India
Coed – Day / Boarding
1,545 Students – Ages 3 to 18
Founded 1984 — RS 2003
www.vivekhighschool.org

Welham Boys' School
Dehra Dun, India
Boys — Day / Boarding
495 Students – Ages 7 to 18
Founded – RS 1996
www.welhamboys.org

Wellington College
Crowthorne, Berkshire, England
Coed – Boarding / Day
705 Students – Ages 13 to 18
Founded 1853 — RS 1995
www.wellington-college.berks.sch.uk

Westfield School
Newcastle upon Tyne, England
Girls – Day
330 Students – Ages 3 to 18
Founded 1960 — RS1992
www.westfield.newcastle.sch.uk

Westminster School
Marion, South Australia
Coed – Day / Boarding
1,071 Students – Ages 5 to 18
Founded 1961 — RS 2001
www.westminster.sa.edu.au

Windermere St. Anne's School
Windermere, Cumbria, England
Coed – Boarding / Day
272 Students – Ages 11 to 18
Founded 1863 — RS 1974
www.wsaschool.com

About the Author

Peter Tacy is Executive Director Emeritus of CAIS, Connecticut Association of Independent Schools, in the USA. Prior to his appointment with CAIS, Peter was Head of Marvelwood School, Connecticut, for eight years and an English teacher and administrator at Buxton School, Massachusetts, for nineteen years. He graduated from Deerfield Academy and Williams College, and did graduate work at Indiana University. A resident for nearly two decades of the old shipbuilding town of Mystic, Connecticut, Peter is an avid sailor, and serves on the Boards of two boating organizations. He is also a former Round Square Board member, and continues to serve as a Trustee of the National Association of Independent Schools (USA). He and his wife Barbara, a clinical psychologist, have two grown sons and two grandchildren.